Primary Gymnastics

A Multi-Activities Approach

Primary Gymnastics

A Multi-Activities Approach

Tansin Benn and Barry Benn

CAMBRIDGE UNIVERSITY PRESS

Published by the Press Syndicate of the University of
Cambridge, The Pitt Building, Trumpington Street,
Cambridge CB2 1RP
40 West 20th Street, New York, NY 10011-4211, USA
10 Stamford Road, Oakleigh, Victoria 3166, Australia

© Cambridge University Press 1992

First published 1992

Printed in Great Britain by Scotprint, Musselburgh,
Scotland

A catalogue record for this book is available from the
British Library

Prepared for publication by
Elizabeth Paren and Gill Stacey
Designed and formatted by Geoffrey Wadsley

ISBN 0 521 40765 6 paperback

Contents

Acknowledgements

There are many people we would like to thank for their support and encouragement in the preparation of this book. Firstly, Jennifer Bird whose patience and constructive comments, through all the drafts of every chapter, proved invaluable. Secondly, David Best, whose friendship and enthusiasm throughout the writing and illustrating period was so much appreciated.

We are grateful to many other people for their willingness to discuss, offer advice, or comment on the approach described in the book: in particular Christine Davies, Dorothy Ledgard, Laura Mund, Marjorie Sheldon, Sue Tims, Rosemary Thompson, Peter Warburton and Hazel Wearmouth.

Finally we would like to thank Malcolm Holmes and the Physical Education Advisory Team in Birmingham for their faith and trust in allowing this new approach to be used on in-service courses from 1985 onwards. Particular thanks are due to Anne Cradock, Yvonne Gandy and Danny Roberts for their direct support and enthusiasm for the approach.

The authors and publishers would like to thank the British Association of Advisers and Lecturers in Physical Education (BAALPE) for their permission for the reproduction of extracts from *Gymnastics in the Secondary School Curriculum* and *Safe Practice in Physical Education*, both available from White Line Publishing Services at 60 Bradford Road, Stanningley, Leeds.

Introduction

This book will be of value to anyone working in the exciting area of gymnastics. The multi-activities approach which it describes has proved successful in several countries and in a range of different situations. The important place given to gymnastics in the National Curriculum for Physical Education in England and Wales, particularly at Key Stages One and Two, ensures that teachers will continue to seek resources in this area. The basis of the multi-activities approach to the teaching of gymnastics is an action-based classification of gymnastic movements which are developed and used to teach performance, planning and evaluation skills. This relates directly to the Programmes of Study and Attainment Targets of the National Curriculum. Consequently, this book will be particularly valuable to teachers planning their gymnastics work in relation to the requirements of the National Curriculum.

It would be inappropriate to embark on this book without attempting to clarify our understanding of the unique value of gymnastics. This view underpins our life-long commitment to the teaching of gymnastics, and provides the motivation for writing this book.

We have been teaching gymnastics for many years in a variety of contexts: as part of a balanced physical education programme in both primary and secondary schools; and on initial and in-service teacher education courses. In addition we are considerably involved with gymnastics in the sporting and recreational contexts and have visited several countries to share our coaching and teaching expertise. All of these experiences have convinced us increasingly of the human values of participation in gymnastics.

As practitioners, we find it hard to translate such values into words but we have seen the self-confidence, movement mastery and understanding that has been achieved by people of all ages and abilities through participation in gymnastics.

In particular we have seen examples of perseverance where individual struggles have achieved success at every level. To cite two examples, we will never forget the day Andrew, suffering from Down's Syndrome, climbed to the top of a five-runged ladder, or the day another Andrew won the British competition which would take him to Russia for a month of sponsored training. Whilst these achievements are not peculiar to gymnastic pursuit, they have encouraged us to try to identify the unique value of gymnastics. Nowhere is this more important than when justifying curriculum areas worthy of inclusion in the education of young children in primary schools.

Alongside dance, games, athletics, swimming and outdoor activities, gymnastics forms part of a well-balanced physical education curriculum. Whilst there are general factors like 'body management' which link the discrete areas of the physical education programme, there are specific factors which make each unique. In gymnastics it is the intrinsic nature of the pursuit of body management skills which is unique. By this we mean that individuals can pursue skill mastery, understanding and concern for the inherent aesthetic potential of human movement, through gymnastic floor and apparatus challenges, for their own sake. This is different from dance where the expressive nature of body management skills and movement understanding can be developed and used creatively for artistic purposes. It is also different from the tactical, co-operative or competitive body management skills pursued through games, and from the specific body management skills required in swimming and adventurous activities.

The intention behind this book is to offer to teachers and students in teacher-training a resource to help them with the teaching of gymnastics in the primary school.

There is nothing in the book which does not work in practice. The multi-activities approach to gymnastics has evolved in the practical situation over a period of ten years. It has been the positive responses from teachers on in-service courses that finally gave us the motivation to produce this book. Teachers have found the content and method recommended in the multi-activities approach accessible and realistic.

The National Curriculum for Physical Education for England and Wales recommends gymnastics as a valued, essential component of a balanced programme of physical education, throughout Key Stages One and Two. This indicates the importance attached to this area as a medium of learning and is consistent with long-held views that gymnastics has a vital contribution to make in this subject, particularly in the movement development of young children.

It is the clarity of focus in gymnastics which makes it central to any physical education programme. More than any other aspect of physical education gymnastics is concerned with individuals realising their own movement potential, striving for quality in movement, and coming to understand the potential of human movement in the most direct way. It may be the very clarity of focus, and the great challenge of individual differences, which has created many of the difficulties for teachers. At the same time, it probably explains why gymnastics has always had a place in physical education, and why it continues to thrive in the community.

There is evidence, for example from Mawer and Head-Rapson (1), which suggests that some students in training receive courses which are too short and inadequate. There are no signs that the pressures which led to this situation will ever be eased, or that the in-service opportunities available will do a great deal to improve teacher confidence in gymnastics teaching (2). Consequently there are some teachers in schools who lack confidence, and pupils who are deprived of consistent experience in this area, or who are often underchallenged. As a result students enter teacher-training courses with insufficient personal experience in gymnastics to provide a basis for their short training courses. This book is offered as an attempt to break that vicious circle, and as a means of support.

It is clear that some teachers, convinced of the value of activities such as gymnastics, need practical help and guidance in teaching the area in order to facilitate the greatest learning potential for their pupils. As is evident from the strong emphasis placed on the development of performance, planning and evaluating skills in this book, we regard the understanding of and integration of these processes in a holistic teaching approach as central to gymnastics in education. However, such process skills cannot be developed in a vacuum: the multi-activities approach specifically places the progressive development of these processes in the gymnastics context.

Historically, some confusion and lack of direction have led to the current need to rethink the teaching of gymnastics in the primary school. The multi-activities approach might help to ensure gymnastics takes its rightful place in the future physical education programme for all children. The experiential nature of gymnastics makes it difficult, or impossible, adequately to express in words, the unique contribution or value gymnastics can make to the development of pupils. Our experience of over twenty years' teaching pupils of all ages and abilities, has shown constant evidence of such value. We have no doubts about the opportunities gymnastics offers for personal challenge, individual success, mastery of movement, understanding of movement and the growth of physical confidence and self-esteem. Every young child should be entitled to enjoy such opportunities.

Tansin Benn
Barry Benn

May 1992

One

A rationale for the multi-activities approach

The current context

For many decades gymnastics in education has suffered controversies and misunderstandings. Yet it has always had a central place in the physical education curriculum. There have been clashes over such issues as teaching methods, the nature of gymnastics, the place of skills in gymnastics, the relationship of community-based sporting gymnastics and gymnastics in education.

During the 1980s the changing views on gymnastics in education emphasised secondary gymnastics. The sporting aspects of gymnastics were flourishing. There were strong developments within a new area of work for the British Amateur Gymnastics Association called recreational or general gymnastics. This extended participation opportunities to people of all ages and abilities.

In education there were more open views on integrating resource material from the rapidly expanding sporting aspects of gymnastics. For example, Bob Smith (3) took a 'holistic' look at gymnastics encompassing sporting and educational categories. He acknowledged that such a perspective may '. . . point the way for teachers to use any aspect of gymnastics if it can be useful for certain children'.

The British Association of Advisers and Lecturers in Physical Education launched *Gymnastics in the Secondary School Curriculum* (4) which offered video and written resource materials for teachers on two approaches to revitalise their secondary physical education programmes: the Skills Approach (Mace and Benn), and the Thematic Areas-of-Skill Approach (John Wright).

When this Secondary Gymnastics Pack was launched in 1988 the lack of new thinking in relation to primary gymnastics was noticeable. In many schools at infant, junior and secondary levels the 'thematic' or educational' approach remained dominant. Gymnastics in the primary schools was certainly still dominated by this approach.

In good hands the thematic approach has been very successful. For less confident teachers it has proved difficult. Evidence such as the 'uneven quality in gymnastics work' found by HMI in the late seventies (5), still persists. As Warburton found (6): 'So often in the case of educational gymnastics there is rarely clear evidence of good quality'.

Finding consensus on suitable themes within the 'educational gymnastics' text-books was difficult. Implementing the thematic approach in schools with inadequate apparatus was unrealistic. For example, attempting to develop a single theme like balance, in a sparsely equipped primary hall, with a class of thirty-five children, would challenge the most imaginative of teachers. There was evidence of little differentiation in teaching ideas or pupils' responses, across the work of infant, junior and secondary children (7).

So, the eighties saw fresh approaches and some consensus in secondary gymnastics. The upsurge in sporting gymnastics was more openly embraced by education. Knowledge was shared, differences and similarities were clearer, and new understandings were reached. It is hoped the future will be a more positive period for primary gymnastics.

The opportunities of gymnastics

Gymnastics can offer particular opportunities for developing:

Performance skills

These involve developing the unique body management skills, with intrinsic aesthetic attention, that constitute gymnastic activity. That means mastering a vocabulary of gymnastic skills related to balancing, rolling, jumping, hanging/swinging/climbing, and taking weight-on-hands.

Planning/composition skills

Gymnastics can also be a vehicle for challenging creative capabilities. From the earliest stages children can be given opportunities to explore, select and formulate movements into sequences, in floor-work, apparatus-work, individually, with partners or groups. Tasks can be made increasingly challenging to develop knowledge, skills and critical appraisal through the gymnastic context.

Evaluating/aesthetic appreciation skills

Since the aesthetic is intrinsic to gymnastic activity, this aspect of physical education can offer an excellent vehicle for the development of aesthetic appreciation. From the first lesson children can be encouraged to experience the satisfaction of doing a movement well, for its own sake. They can be guided to look critically at their own work and that of others. Teachers can help children to find the language to describe movement, to identify features of good performance such as form, line, shape and continuity.

Eventually pupils will be able to make informed value-judgements on their own work and that of others. They will become discerning adults, able to appreciate human movement potential and achievement.

Social skills

For children to maximise the learning potential of gymnastics in education they must be able to assume a personal and communal responsibility. For safe practice in gymnastics there must be shared responsibility in relation to behaviour, safety and caring for others. As the children mature and are able to assume more responsibility gymnastics can facilitate many ways of furthering social skills, for example in moving apparatus, in supporting each other's body weight in simple skills, in creating sequences with partners or groups, in planning apparatus designs, and in co-operative learning situations (8).

Health and fitness knowledge

There are many aspects related to health and fitness that can be learned through gymnastics, for example:

1 Gymnastics offers a particular opportunity to focus attention on the fitness aspects of strength and flexibility; by participating, and through focused observation, children will learn to understand the importance of these factors in skilful body management, and to appreciate individual differences and their effects.
2 Children need to understand that safe progression in skill-learning must relate to sound physical preparation, for example good body tension is vital for balancing skills and there are certain exercises, for particular muscle groups, that will develop this body tension.
3 The value of good body posture, an essential ingredient of gymnastic movement, can be appropriately in focus in this aspect of the curriculum. Good body posture is a life-skill, as are other important health factors that can be taught through gymnastics such as the principles of safe lifting.

Extending knowledge and understanding of movement

Teachers could use learning in the gymnastic context to relate associated movement principles. The following two examples offer suggestions:

1 Scientific principles involved in the mechanics of balance or rotation could be taught as the children experience these phenomena.
2 Movement principles (called 'supporting concepts' in this book) can be introduced to extend understanding of the

variety and complexity of human movement. These include: changing body shape, use of different body parts, changing the direction of a movement, the pathway of a series of movements, the speed of a movement or the level at which a movement occurs.

Development of the multi-activities approach

The multi-activities approach offers the possibility of a fresh teaching method for gymnastics in the primary school. The authors started work on this approach in a community recreational gymnastics programme for young children in 1980. The principles continue in that programme today. The authors are no less stringent about the 'why, what and how' of gymnastics for young children in community programmes than they are for gymnastics in education. Since 1985 the multi-activities approach has been further developed and refined in the educational context of colleges and schools. The positive responses of students and teachers suggest we should be optimistic for the future of gymnastics in the primary schools. It is hoped that the multi-activities approach will help pupils to obtain more equal and consistent access to gymnastics within the balanced physical education programme required by the National Curriculum.

The multi-activities approach differs from other methods in:
  ◇ its action classification of gymnastic activity
  ◇ in the recommended application of that classification to the teaching situation

Classification

Consistent with the requirements of the National Curriculum Key Stages One and Two Programmes of Study, five action categories are recognised as central to gymnastic experience and potential development in this area:
  1 Jumping
  2 Rolling
  3 Balancing
  4 Hanging/swinging/climbing (those activities in which body weight is suspended by the upper body)
  5 Taking weight-on-hands (those inversion activities in which the body weight is supported by the upper body)

Photographs 1–3 show movements related to each of the five activity categories.

Application

It is recommended that children experience all five types of movement within every lesson. For example, a warm-up might involve an enjoyable, vigorous jumping activity.

Floor-work might develop balancing skills, perhaps linking

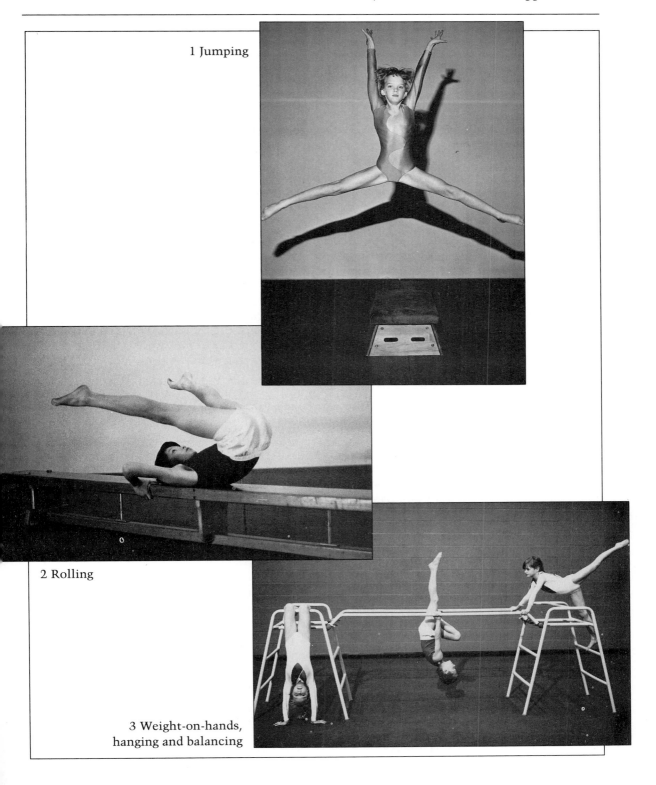

1 Jumping

2 Rolling

3 Weight-on-hands,
hanging and balancing

balances in sequences. For the culminating apparatus part of the lesson the equipment could be structured to facilitate a major action category at each apparatus station. As an example there could be a bench station for continuing the balancing ideas, an inclined padded plank for rolling, a circle of hoops to continue jumping skills, the climbing frame with linking poles for hanging/swinging/climbing, and wooden planks for weight-on-hands activities. In groups the children would spend some time at each station before rotating onto the next. As part of a planned scheme of work this type of lesson would ensure:

- ✧ variety and interest for the learner
- ✧ ongoing development of movement confidence and skill level within the five action categories
- ✧ appropriate, well-balanced physical demands on young, growing bodies

Suitability

Within the approach there is potential for developing a school policy on gymnastics which suits the needs of children across the nursery to junior years age range. At the nursery end apparatus and activities can be designed to encourage movements within the five action categories. At this stage the children should be given the freedom to explore and choose their movement responses with sensitive, appropriate intervention from teachers. Within the more structured programme of the infant and junior years the multi-activities approach enables children to develop:

- ✧ performance, planning/composition, and evaluation/ appreciation skills from direct involvement with practical gymnastic experiences
- ✧ knowledge and understanding about this aspect of human movement potential
- ✧ positive and responsible attitudes towards caring for themselves and each other through participation in a good gymnastics programme

An action-based curriculum

The multi-activities approach to primary gymnastics offers an action-based curriculum. Teachers have attributed the following features to its success:

- ✧ a clear rationale offering a structure on which to develop gymnastic learning experiences for children
- ✧ realistic apparatus demands which can be exciting and purposeful even with limited resources
- ✧ built-in variety of movement experiences which sustains the interest, concentration and physical resources of young children
- ✧ a sound foundation programme which facilitates movement

confidence and competence, enabling safe progression in skill-learning

Ten principles for a teaching approach

In 1988, BAALPE, the British Association of Advisers and Lecturers in Physical Education, produced a booklet and video called *Gymnastics in the Secondary School Curriculum*. In the booklet ten principles were identified which should be reflected in any teaching approach to curriculum gymnastics. They are considered so fundamental to the teaching of gymnastics, for any age group, that they are outlined here. The essence of these principles underpins the multi-activities approach as strongly as it underpinned the recommended secondary approaches.

1 Gymnastics is concerned with the development and balanced use of the body's physical resources–particularly muscular strength and flexibility.

This is reflected through the action classification of the multi-activities approach, through the recommendation that every lesson includes some activity in each action category, and in the recognised importance of body preparation (see Chapter 11).

2 Gymnastics is concerned with some of the aesthetic aspects of human movement.

Through the multi-activities approach the central aesthetic nature of gymnastics is recognised. The development of increasingly complex evaluation skills, in particular skills of aesthetic appreciation, is central to the teaching of this approach (see Chapter 6).

3 Gymnastics is concerned with the development of skill.

Teaching the multi-activities approach involves the development of performance skills, planning/composition skills, and evaluation/appreciation skills. Suggestions for ways in which all three might be achieved are made in Chapters 4, 5 and 6 respectively. The intention is that performance is the core of learning and that the other skills of composition and appreciation are developed through performance. The processes are dealt with separately in the first part of the book for clarity. The latter part of the book illustrates ways in which all three skill areas are integrated in a holistic approach to good teaching in primary gymnastics.

4 Gymnastics is concerned with the development of knowledge and understanding.

Through the multi-activities approach pupils are encouraged to develop their understanding of the potential of human movement in the gymnastics context. This is achieved through involving pupils in a range of processes including observing, sharing, creating, planning, questioning and discussing.

5 Gymnastics provides the optimum educational potential when it is used to foster individuality, cater for special needs and foster co-operative social behaviour.

The multi-activities approach offers teachers the opportunity to foster individuality through the breadth of the movement classification, and the scope of responses within each action category. There are many suggestions for encouraging co-operative social behaviour in the book, for example in safe sharing of apparatus, in helping each other to move apparatus, in working with others on performance, planning and evaluation skills.

6 Gymnastics requires a variety of teaching and learning procedures.

Teacher sensitivity, awareness, observation skills and ability to use a range of teaching styles, will all complement good teaching in gymnastics. The multi-activities approach demands flexible use of teaching styles, for example directed, guided-discovery, open-ended, reciprocal. Examples of these are suggested in Chapter 3.

7 Gymnastics should be pupil-success orientated.

Using the multi-activities approach teachers can organise learning in a structured, progressive, appropriate manner to facilitate successful experiences for pupils. However, the success of the approach is dependent on the skill and sensitivity of the teacher, in recognising the needs of the children.

8 Gymnastic programmes should reflect a balance between floor and apparatus work.

In the multi-activities approach it is recommended that every lesson includes both floor-work and apparatus-work. For infant children a bias towards apparatus time is recommended, with a more even balance of time as the children develop the abilities to practise and repeat more refined floor-work skills in their junior years. It is recognised that this is not always possible but a balance over each half-term block of work is strongly recommended.

9 Gymnastics should be planned and taught with proper regard for progression.

Chapters 4, 5 and 6 which deal with the development of performance, planning/composition and evaluation/appreciation skills offer guidance on structuring progressive learning within the multi-activities approach. Chapter 8 includes a suggested half-term unit of work for each primary year group from reception to year six. The purpose is to indicate the potential for progression across the age range using this approach.

10 Gymnastics should be taught with constant reference to safety procedures.

Concern for safety and safe teaching in gymnastics permeates the book. There are illustrations of safe techniques, correct supports and recommended safe progressions. Chapter 10 is specifically concerned with safety in teaching gymnastics.

The evidence of support for these ten under-pinning principles suggested by BAALPE, outlined above, can be found throughout this book.

Two

Understanding the multi-activities approach

The multi-activities approach to gymnastics offers a realistic and accessible methodology for teaching and learning gymnastics through the primary years. Within the approach there is scope for nursery departments to structure situations which encourage the early exploration of fundamental gymnastic activities, and the opportunity for top primary children to satisfy their desire for more refined skill mastery within the identified activity areas. The approach facilitates the integrated development of performance, planning and evaluation skills in the context of gymnastics. In this context the child has the opportunity to extend and refine body management skills for their own sake, and to experience the unique challenge of this aspect of physical education.

After many years of gymnastics teaching in a variety of situations and with people of all ages and abilities, the authors have come to appreciate that gymnastics can be seen as a continuum that has its roots in play and its ultimate sophistication in the forms of sports acrobatics, artistic and rhythmic gymnastics. In the primary school gymnastics capitalises on the child's innate urge to explore movement for its own sake. Natural childhood experiences often involve self-challenge. Most children, through play, find an inherent delight in situations requiring rolling, jumping, balancing, swinging or turning upside down. These actions form the basis of the categories used in this multi-activities approach to gymnastics. In play children often repeat these movements for the sheer pleasure of the experience or for finding new levels of success and movement mastery. The physical education programme in schools fosters and develops such motivation through structured, safe teaching. This enables pupils to continue learning about themselves and their physical capabilities in relation to the world around them.

Consequently, gymnastics, more than any other area of physical education, builds on the basic drive to explore movement activities for their own sake, and to achieve new personal levels of success at all ages and stages of development.

The suggestions made in this book are intended to offer a framework and guidance to teachers. Application of the approach requires flexibility in method as teachers respond to the needs of their pupils and the specific opportunities of their situations. For example, a range of teaching styles will be required to ensure pupils realise their full potential in gymnastics. There will be times when the teacher will need to encourage exploration of activities and other occasions when more specific skill guidance is essential to safety, success and progression. Another example of the need for flexibility of teaching approach might relate to the introduction of more complex gymnastic skills and ideas such as partner-work or use of music. Judgements about appropriate timing of these introductions can only be made by the informed, sensitive teacher who constantly responds to the achievements and needs of his or her pupils.

Classifications of movement

The multi-activities approach uses two important movement classifications.

The central one is the **activities classification** which lists five types of action which encompass the most basic to the most complex skill-learning in gymnastics. Within each category there is potential for the development of many related gymnastic movement patterns.

The second classification of **supporting movement concepts** is the means by which gymnastic movement can have infinite variety and development.

The activities classification

1 Balancing
2 Jumping
3 Swinging, hanging, climbing (or those activities in which the body weight is suspended partially or wholly by the upper body)
4 Rolling
5 Taking weight-on-hands (or those activities in which the body weight is supported partially or wholly by the upper body)

The following apparatus examples illustrate the range of potential experiences that can develop from this classification.

Example one

A reception class has an 'exploratory' apparatus lay-out. This encourages, during the pupils' rotation around the stations, general differentiation of movement patterns in line with the gymnastic activities classification. Fig 1 shows the 'circuit' nature of each station, designed to help the young children to stay at their stations until rotated by the teacher. The 'circuit' also maximises activity time. This apparatus lay-out would be suitable for 15–20 children.

balancing

jumping

rolling

taking weight-on-hands

hanging/swinging/climbing

Fig 1   Apparatus for encouraging movements within the five activity categories

Example two

In a top junior class pupils are working on a partner apparatus sequence, to include skills from any two of the five categories. Fig 2 on page 14 shows how the apparatus lay-out is designed to enable partner-work to occur at each station. A comfortable class size for this lay-out would be 28 children.

The classification of activities offers teachers a means of structuring, analysing and evaluating learning through the gymnastics context. The most important feature is that the categories are action based and encompass the widest range of gymnastic movement patterns. Initially young children will develop general movement confidence and familiarisation with the range of experiences in the classification. As they revisit these movement experiences they will seek to broaden their movement vocabulary, improve their understanding and refine their skill mastery.

There are many ways in which each category of activity can be varied, developed, combined and extended to offer pupils interesting and progressive learning opportunities throughout the primary years. Performance, planning and evaluation skills can all be developed through this approach. For example, the classification enables teachers to clarify the monitoring of performance skills such as breadth of movement vocabulary and level of skill, by relating movements observed to the five action categories. Within each category there are clearly related skilful movement patterns, or 'families of skills', which enable the teacher to recognise and assess progress. In order to facilitate a systematic approach to broadening movement vocabulary and understanding, a range of supporting movement concepts is suggested.

Supporting movement concepts

This term refers to aspects of movement which are not action based but which can be applied to action tasks to bring about change and therefore variation in those actions.

The supporting movement concepts are:
- body parts
- shape
- time
- direction
- level
- pathway

An example of applying one concept to an action task would be:
Try to roll (action), *in different body shapes* (supporting concept). *You might try a stretched roll, a tucked roll, or one which changes from stretched to tucked.*

Initially young children, or those with little gymnastic experience, will need to gain some control and mastery of movement patterns within the five fundamental activity

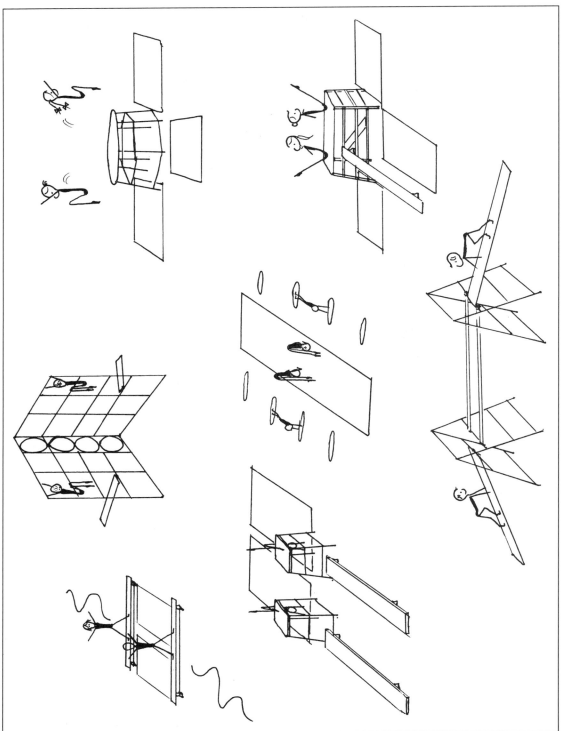

Fig 2   Apparatus for partner-work

categories. After this stage pupils will find stimulating and challenging variety through the phased introduction of a range of concepts that can be applied to the basic activities. They are referred to as supporting movement concepts since the intention is to use them to support and extend pupil response to an action task. Used in this way there is infinite potential for increasing movement vocabulary.

Through the phased application of the supporting concepts the children will learn:

◇ that the body can move on different parts
◇ that the body can change shape
◇ that the body can move at different speeds
◇ that the body can move into different directions
◇ that the body can move along different pathways
◇ that the body can move at different levels

Once pupils start to explore supporting concepts in relation to the gymnastic activity categories, they will find a wealth of movement responses. Encouraging the development of such a movement vocabulary is essential to sequence work in which composition skills are vital. Linking movements together in increasingly challenging ways can have very simple beginnings. For example an early combination of linking action and supporting concepts in a sequence task might be:

Join two rolls which move into different directions.

Later the actions and supporting concepts can be combined with increasing complexity:

Make up a sequence of a roll, a jump and a balance, which shows three different body shapes and a clear change of speed.

As illustrated through these examples the level of complexity in sequence skills can be built progressively as the children learn more about movement and the skills of planning or composition. These skills can be developed from an early age and might include:

◇ creating skilful and accurate responses to tasks
◇ exploring new ideas
◇ selecting and synthesising material
◇ aiming for originality
◇ remembering and practising increasingly complex patterns
◇ negotiating and adapting to working with others

Such skills are necessarily directly related to performing and offer increasingly complex opportunities for evaluation. Planning sequences, or the development of composition skills, is considered in more depth in Chapter 5 (page 50). Teachers can help pupils with evaluation skills by nurturing their understanding of movement through this perspective. For example observation and discussion skills can be focused around gymnastic movement from the first lesson. Finding a language for movement, developing a critical awareness of high quality movement, encouraging informed value-judgements in this area of aesthetic education, are all skills that develop naturally alongside performance and composition skills in gymnastics. The area of evaluation related to aesthetic appreciation skills is considered in more depth in Chapter 6 (page 61).

Three

Teaching the multi-activities approach

This chapter contains general guidelines on teaching method using the multi-activities approach. As in all curriculum areas there will be differences in method as individual teachers use their particular knowledge, time and resources in response to their pupils' needs. The suggestions here only illustrate ways in which the basic premise of approach can be managed, ensuring that pupils have regular and developmental movement experiences in the five activity areas of balancing, jumping, rolling, taking weight-on-hands, and hanging/swinging/ climbing.

It is recommended that in each school there should be a whole-school policy for gymnastics, as in other subject areas, to ensure curriculum consistency and continuity. Therefore it is proposed that staff should negotiate a policy for gymnastics specific to the time, facilities and expertise within their school. Developing a school policy for gymnastics is discussed in more detail in Chapter 7.

Within a whole-school policy for gymnastics the multi-activities approach can result in the gradual, parallel development of a wide range of knowledge and skills. The approach involves pupils experiencing some aspect of all five activity categories within every gymnastics lesson.

This variety and contrast in movement challenges can be particularly successful in the primary context. Pupils make good progress in skill learning through short, regular experiences in the different activity categories. Skill patterns develop in parallel ensuring a physically sound programme, which avoids over-use of muscle groups and related fatigue. Progressive skill refinement is nurtured as activity categories are revisited with increasing task complexity, competence and understanding.

This approach, with its variety of activities, is also realistic, in management terms, for most primary schools, including those with large classes and limited apparatus. For instance it is not difficult to design an apparatus plan which facilitates a range of activities with one station for balancing, one for jumping, one for climbing, one for rolling etc. In contrast designing a plan to enable all pupils to experience a single type of action such as balance, which might be required in a thematic approach, is often impossible in poorly equipped primary schools.

As children become more experienced and move through the primary years the basic premise of the approach remains unchanged. However, teachers can be more flexible, expanding and developing areas of work in relation to pupils' increasing abilities to understand movement concepts and master finer skills.

Examples of how the multi-activities approach can be introduced and developed are shown in the following lesson analysis, and in the sample lesson plans at the end of the chapter for classes aged four, seven and ten years.

Lesson analysis

This example of a lesson format illustrates how the range of activities can be incorporated within one lesson. The common lesson format of introduction/warm-up, development of floor-work, apparatus work and conclusion is used.

1 Introduction/warm-up

The warm-up and introduction should provide a vigorous and enjoyable start to the lesson, thus increasing the children's motivation for what follows. Where possible the warm-up should lay the foundations for the work that is to follow. Both the start and end of lessons are useful times for concentrating on strength and flexibility. Setting related tasks as introductory and concluding activities can be helpful in reinforcing the importance of body preparation. Ideas for developing this aspect are suggested in Chapter 11.

2 Floor-work

Floor-work should focus on one of the fundamental activities, supporting concepts, or more complex combinations depending on age and stage of development.

The teacher can approach the use of floor-work time in many different ways. In early stages the children might need help mastering basic actions within an activity category such as 'jumping'. This could involve paying attention to related skills such as hopping, skipping, leaping. Later on, pupils can be challenged by applying a supporting concept such as changing 'body shape' to their skills. Another stage might involve technical help with a specific skill to facilitate success and understanding. The concept of sequence work might be introduced during floor-work time and later partner-work ideas. So floor-work time offers an opportunity to focus pupils' attention on an aspect of gymnastics, appropriate to pupils' needs, in order to improve knowledge, understanding and/or skill level.

3 Apparatus

Apparatus time can also be used flexibly but essentially the apparatus plan or lay-out is designed to stimulate all five basic activities as the children rotate around the stations (see Fig 1 on page 12).

Initially the children will enjoy spending a short time at each station and rotating around activities. For example, it might be possible to move them around five stations in a thirty minute lesson. As they get older pupils will need more time at each station to practise and consolidate skills. It might be more appropriate to move half the stations one week and the other half the following week. The principle remains the same, that is to offer pupils frequent experiences over the range of activities.

A new apparatus lay-out every half-term has proved most successful in the early years. The short but regular opportunity to explore the challenges at each station enables the children to become familiar with the lay-out, to assimilate ideas, to experiment with, practise and repeat movement patterns. With imagination it is not difficult to produce a number of multi-activities apparatus plans for successive half-term periods, even with limited equipment. Plans should take into account progression in relation to heights and widths of apparatus and the need for increasingly complex combinations.

Work on the apparatus should relate to floor-work in some way. For example, balancing ideas on the floor can be extended on the balancing station in the apparatus circuit, still enabling the other varied activity stations to extend further the children's learning. Sequence work or partner activities on the floor might also be extended within the same lesson on the apparatus.

(Figs 3–7, starting on page 20, show examples of applying supporting concepts to activity categories in floor-work and apparatus tasks.)

4 Conclusion

Finishing a lesson purposefully is important and there are many ways in which this can be done. The method selected in each lesson will depend on what has been happening in that lesson and the teacher's perception of it. The conclusion could be used, for example:

- ⬥ as a calming activity, following a particularly vigorous or exciting lesson
- ⬥ to reinforce something positive that occurred in the lesson
- ⬥ to remind pupils about important safety factors or points of technique, covered during the lesson
- ⬥ to question or discuss an aspect of the lesson
- ⬥ to highlight any special successes

Relationship between lesson phases

Regular and developmental experiences of movement patterns, based on the five activity categories of this approach, will ensure

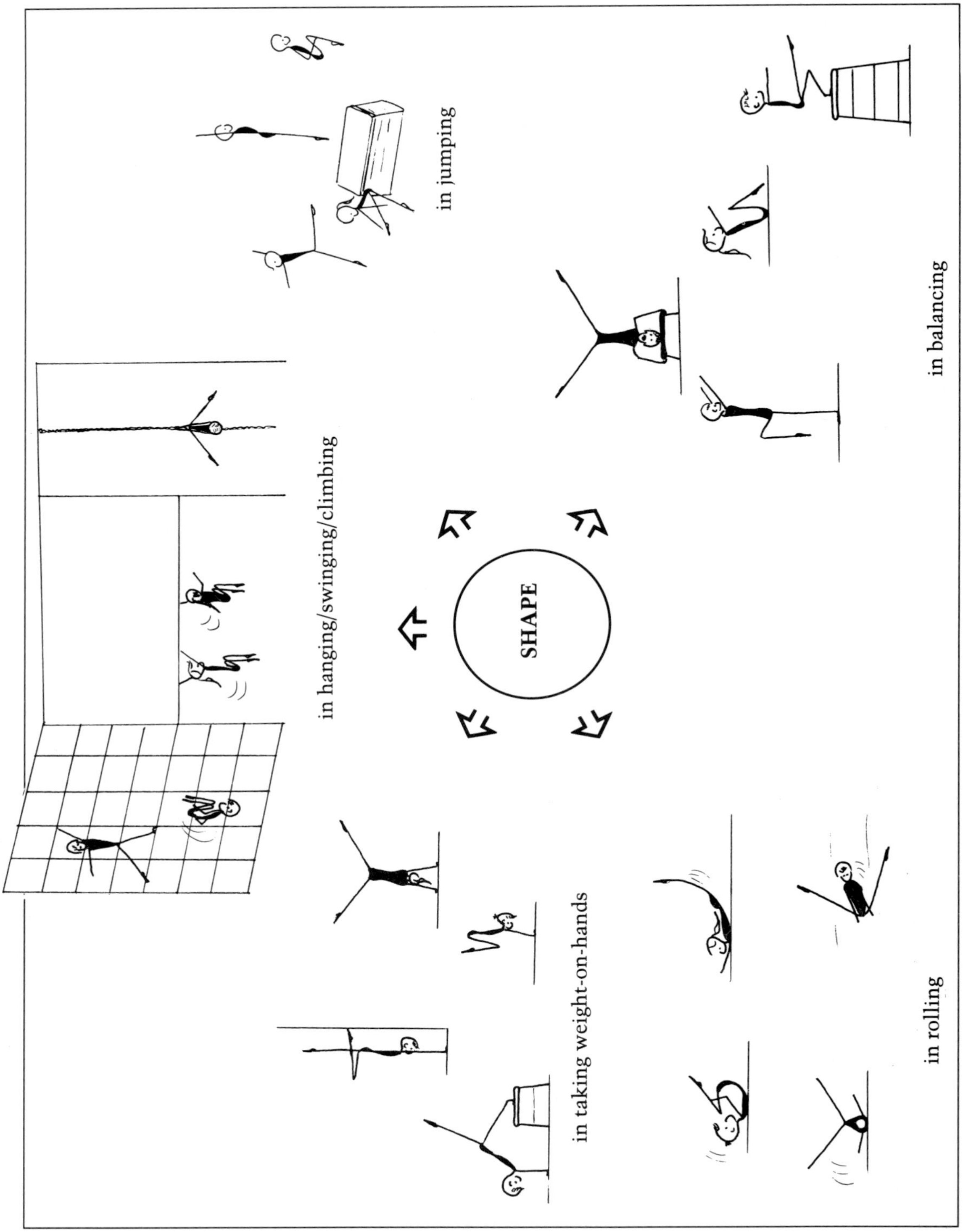

Fig 3   Applying changes in shape to activity categories

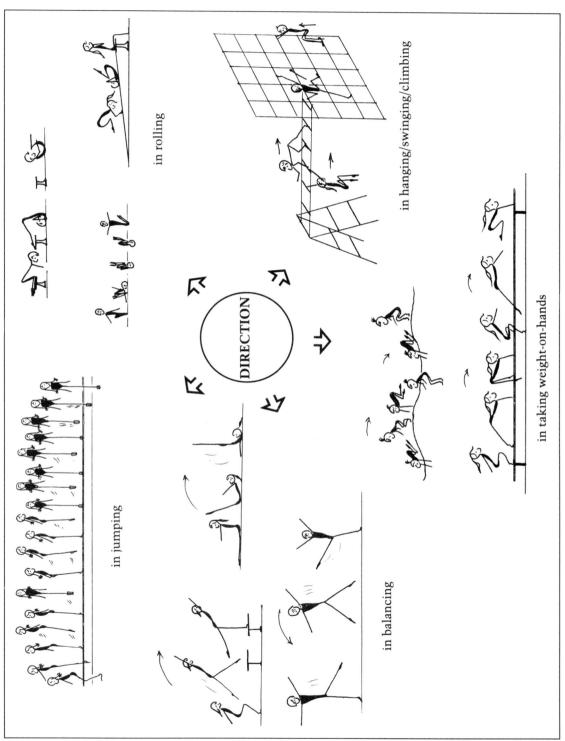

Fig 4 Applying changes in direction to activity categories

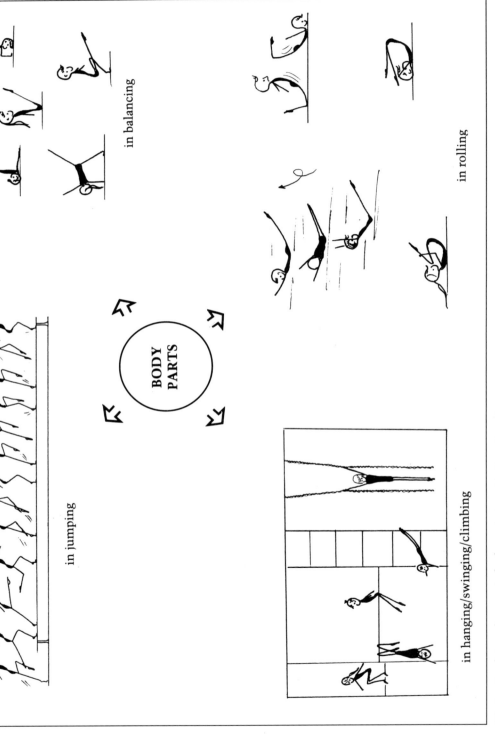

in balancing

in rolling

in jumping

BODY PARTS

in hanging/swinging/climbing

Fig 5   Applying changes in body parts to activity categories

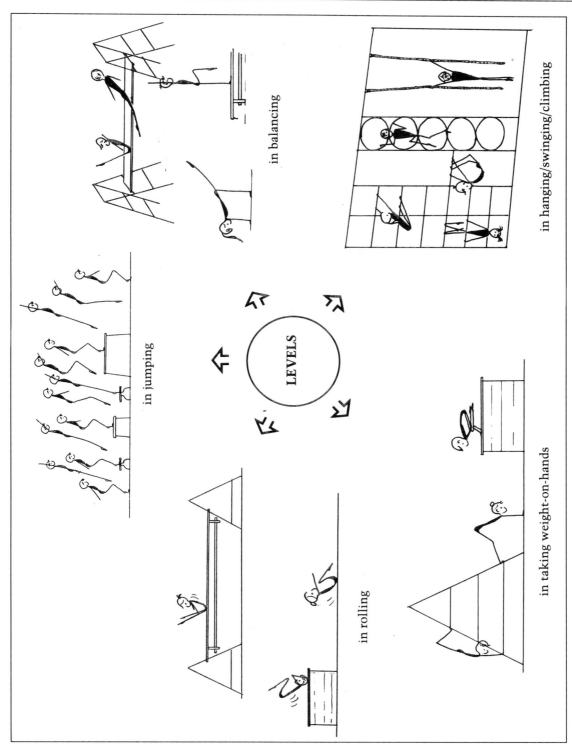

Fig 6 Applying changes in level to activity categories

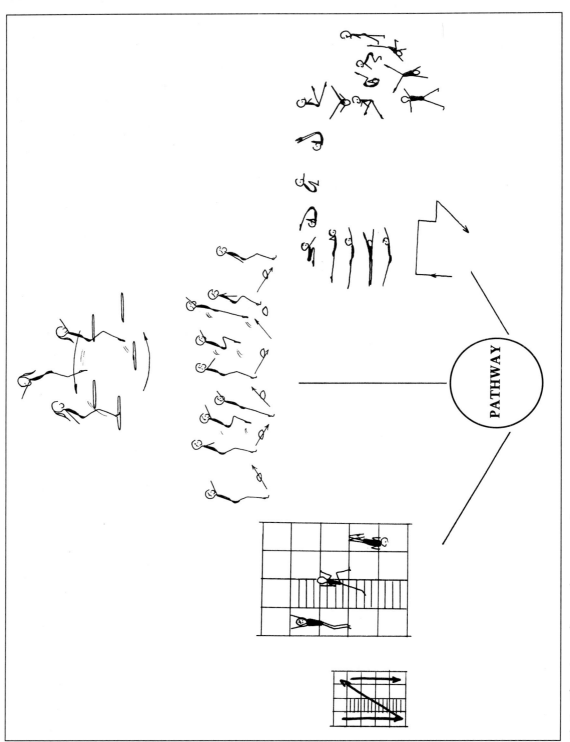

Fig 7   Changing pathway when sequencing movements

continuity between lessons. There should also be continuity within lessons. For example, pupils will develop a vocabulary of skills on the floor. Related skills are reinforced, further challenged and extended on the apparatus. Families of related skills, within each activity category, will gradually be identified and mastered as pupils progressively challenge themselves within the five activity categories. In another example, using the application of supporting concepts to basic activities, the pupils could contrast changing body shape in jumping during floor-work with changing body shape whilst performing all activities on their apparatus circuit.

Adapting teaching method

Clearly the challenge within this approach changes as the pupils progress and the teacher develops the floor-work and apparatus tasks, as well as the environment itself through new apparatus plans. As pupils develop confidence and competence through regular experiences of a range of activities, the teacher can adapt his/her teaching method in different ways.

There will come a time when pupils need longer periods to explore, select, repeat, practise and refine more complex skill challenges. They might want to spend a whole lesson on developing a floor-work sequence, whilst a longer time on apparatus might be required a week later. Teachers should be free to adjust time according to pupils' needs, as long as the overall balance between floor and apparatus time is maintained. It is suggested that the younger children would benefit most from a bias towards apparatus time, whilst older pupils respond positively to an even balance between floor and apparatus time as concentration spans and physical abilities develop.

Being flexible about teaching styles will also add interest, variety and challenge to gymnastic lessons. For instance there will be times when tasks related to exploration and guided discovery of movement experiences are most appropriate, for example:

Taking your weight on your hands move across and along your bench.

There will be other times when specific skill teaching, with progressive lead-up stages, needs to be introduced in a very direct manner. For example when a group is ready to learn the cartwheel, the bench can be used for very specific weight-on-hands progressions which will help with this specific skill (see Fig 8).

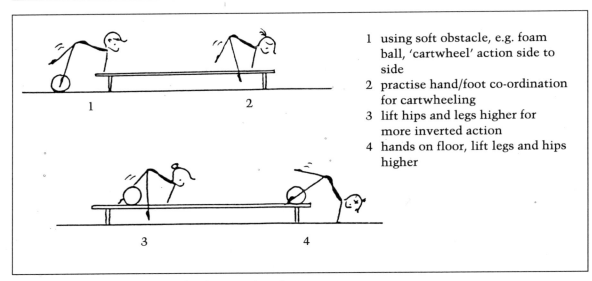

1 using soft obstacle, e.g. foam ball, 'cartwheel' action side to side
2 practise hand/foot co-ordination for cartwheeling
3 lift hips and legs higher for more inverted action
4 hands on floor, lift legs and hips higher

Fig 8   Progressions for a cartwheel using a bench

On other occasions young children might benefit from reciprocal teaching, with one pupil assisting a partner through close observation and analysis. Helping the 'pupil teacher' to see and communicate positive and constructive comments can be demanding on the class teacher, but it is a very real means of increasing knowledge and developing understanding and social skills in pupils.

Finally, the importance of training children to lift, carry and place apparatus safely is also an integral part of gymnastics. This necessitates very tightly controlled instructions and responses.

Sample lesson plan 1

Age: 4 years, second term
Time: 25 minutes
Number in class: 24
Aim: To increase vocabulary of movement patterns in the five activity categories.
Objectives: By the end of the lesson the children will have:
 ✧ understood and improved their landings from jumps
 ✧ improved their performance of the bunny jump skill
 ✧ enjoyed responding to music through different movement challenges
 ✧ experimented with a range of movement patterns on the apparatus circuit structured
   to encourage movements from the five activity categories
 ✧ observed and discussed peer work in relation to quality and diversity

Activity	Teaching points	Organisation/Strategies
INTRODUCTION		
'Musical jumps' Jump on the spot to the music, sit down when it stops. 'Musical hops' Hopping on one leg, change legs after each stop.	Bend knees to land. Put heels down on landing. Jumping higher and higher. Stretch toes in the air. Keep backs straight.	Individual spaces.
FLOOR-WORK		
Hands on floor lifting one leg then the other into the air. 'Bunny jumps' Hands on floor jump bottoms into the air.	Stretch leg towards ceiling. Long toes. Look at hands. Keep arms straight. Knees stay bent.	Good pupil demonstration.

Sit in 6 groups of 4.   Pupils assist with the moving of small apparatus where possible.

APPARATUS		
Allocate groups to stations. Remind pupils of activity focus/station. 1 Jumping 2 Balancing 3 Taking weight-on-hands 4 Hanging/swinging/climbing 5 Rolling 6 Free activity	We are looking for good work and different ideas today, to show each other. Don't forget to bend those knees as you land from your jumps and keep those arms straight in your bunny jumps.	Demonstrations and discussion as appropriate. Rotate around stations about every 3 minutes.

Tidy away small apparatus.

CONCLUSION		
'Musical statues' Jumping or hopping to the music, freeze when it stops. 'Musical balances' Questioning about landings from jumps and safe bunny jumping.	Hold very still. Listen carefully to the music. On stopping show a balance that is very still. Use any of the balances you tried on the balancing station today.	Own spaces.

Sample lesson plan 2

Age: 7–8 years
Time: 30 minutes
Number in class: 32
Aim: To increase vocabulary of movement patterns by applying the supporting concept of shape to work within the five activity categories.
Objectives: By the end of the lesson the children will have:

- ✧ experienced a range of activities whilst trying to apply the concept of changing body shape
- ✧ learnt a teacher directed sequence built around jumping with different body shapes
- ✧ explored a range of balances aiming to show changes of shape
- ✧ selected, and linked three balances into their own sequences
- ✧ observed and discussed peer work in relation to quality and attention to shape

Activity	*Teaching points*	*Organisation/Strategies*
INTRODUCTION Develop jumping sequence to music. 3 jumps tuck jump, 3 jumps star jump. Jump to crouch, stretch to front support hold, jump to crouch, stretched jump. Repeat.	Look for clear shapes, good stretch, wide in star jump and long on straight jump. Front support position must be straight and still.	Build sequence one section at a time. Introduce music after tuck/star jump stage. Own spaces.
FLOOR-WORK Balances–ask to see some balances which have different body shapes. Tell pupils to choose three balances which have very different shapes and see if they can join them in a sequence. Ask all Number 1s to show the best sequence they can. Change over.	Think about shapes you have just made in your jumps: can you use the same ideas? Look for clear shapes, smooth joins in sequence; good starting and finishing positions. Number 2s watch partner closely, to see the three balances and to check if each has different shape.	Share a range of ideas as they emerge. Observe and discuss good examples. Arrange in pairs.

Sit in 8 groups of 4.   Arrange apparatus as required.

APPARATUS Allocate groups to stations. Remind pupils of activity focus/station: 1 jumping (any) 2 balancing 3 taking weight-on-hands 4 hanging/swinging 5 rolling 6 tuck, star and straight jumps with good landings (box top) 7 climbing 8 combination of activities	Think about the changing body shape while working on each activity station. I am looking for any really good work and unusual ideas.	Demonstrate and discuss as appropriate. Rotate around 4 stations every 4 minutes (other 4 stations next week). Pupils need to remember where they finish. Class leaders mark on classroom model. Clear apparatus as required.
CONCLUSION Ask pupils to remember balancing sequence they made up at start of lesson and ask them to tell you the most important thing they were asked to show in their balances.	Work very quietly so that you can concentrate. Show each balance before moving into next one. Remember your sequence so that you can practise it again next week.	Own spaces.

Sample lesson plan 3

Age: 10 years
Time: 40 minutes
Number in class: 32
Aim: To encourage co-operative skills as the children start to explore a range of partner work ideas.
Objectives: By the end of the lesson the children will have:
- ✧ explored matching, mirroring and follow the leader partner ideas in relation to balancing, jumping and rolling on the floor
- ✧ been through processes of sharing, communicating, negotiating, adapting and sensitising responses to a partner
- ✧ extended these skills through exploration of the same three partner ideas in relation to all five activity categories on apparatus

Activity	*Teaching points*	*Organisation/Strategies*
INTRODUCTION		
Jogging round room. When you call out number pupils sit back to back in groups that size. With last partner, pupils test each other's body tension with 'Stubborn Mule Game'. Change over roles.	Look for a quick response to the number called. 'Stubborn Mule Game' – Number 1 stands with hands and feet wide apart. Tries not to be pushed over by Number 2.	Vary the number between 2 and 7. Finish with 2. In 2s in spaces.
FLOOR-WORK		
Tell pupils to use same tension to find balances which they can match with partner. Then to try some jumps, using partner as a mirror. Finally get them to try rolling, following partner across mat to illustrate 'canon'.	Look for careful matching: the same shapes must be held for the same amount of time. How would your partner's balance have to change to look like your balance reflected in a mirror? Can you time your jumps to be exactly in unison? Choose rolls which you can both do well.	Mats out as names are called.

Partners to join with another 2 to make groups of 4.

Activity	*Teaching points*	*Organisation/Strategies*
APPARATUS		
Allocate groups to stations. Plan apparatus to extend partner ideas in 1 balancing 2 taking weight-on-hands 3 hanging/swinging/climbing 4 jumping and rolling	Pupils need to think about possibilities for matching, mirroring or following the leader, while on activity stations. Partners should discuss the skills they both feel able to try.	Demonstrate and discuss as appropriate. Rotate around 4 stations about every 5 minutes.

Clear apparatus as required.

Activity	*Teaching points*	*Organisation/Strategies*
CONCLUSION		
Ask pupils to move into a space and sit in straddle fold position. Tell them they can continue their partner-work ideas next week and will have longer time on one piece of apparatus to explore more ideas.	Relax so that your tummies move nearer to the floor: keep legs straight as possible.	Own spaces.

Four

Developing performance skills

It is hoped that the classification of movement into different categories will provide a clearer structure for planning and developing gymnastic activities. The use of categories assists with structuring schemes, lessons and apparatus situations. In this chapter the five activity categories will be used to consider a range of suggestions for developing performance skills in gymnastics.

Teachers need to recognise achievement and have the knowledge to develop movement potential. Such knowledge will help pupils towards greater understanding and skill refinement. Equally, when pupils are not achieving their desired movement pattern, teachers need to be aware of easier stages in the learning process.

The three stages of development considered in this chapter are:
1 Becoming familiar with basic activities within the classification.
2 Broadening movement vocabulary through applying the supporting concepts.
3 Refining movement patterns to improve skills.

The stages are not necessarily sequential. For instance, teachers might need to offer technical help, to improve skill refinement, at a very early stage. An example might be when a child is unsuccessfully attempting forward rolls on the rolling station. Some advice from the teacher about tucking the chin onto the chest, to make the back more curved, could help the child to succeed with the skill. It will certainly ensure a safer movement pattern.

Becoming familiar with basic activities

At this stage children are learning to differentiate movement patterns within the five activity categories: jumping, balancing, taking weight-on-hands, rolling, hanging/ swinging /climbing. Appropriate apparatus stations and general but clear tasks will encourage this learning, for example:

This apparatus station is for rolling.

Fig 1 on page 12 offers some suggestions for structuring early apparatus experiences in each of the five areas. At this stage children should be encouraged to explore a range of related activities without specific skill demands. For example, an apparatus station designed to stimulate jumping activities should be briefly introduced to the class as 'for jumping.' Diversity of pupil response related to jumping, perhaps hopping or jumping sideways, should be praised. Responses that are outside of the jumping task, for example pupils balancing or rolling, should be discouraged with explanation.

It is clear from Fig 1 that one station per activity category is usually required. With this approach it is suggested that the apparatus lay-out is initially changed every half-term. Change of apparatus will stimulate different movement responses. On re-designing an apparatus lay-out the teacher can use his or her imagination to design stations to encourage progressive movement responses in the five activity categories. Opportunity for progression and variety can be offered through changing the types of apparatus, the heights, combinations, surfaces or spaces between pieces of apparatus. For example, to stimulate variety and progression in jumping experiences the teacher could use:

- ✧ small obstacles on the floor for jumping over e.g. bean bags, skipping ropes
- ✧ hoops for jumping in and out, or around
- ✧ a plank on the floor to offer a narrower surface for jumping along, over, on/off, across
- ✧ obstacles on the plank for more complex negotiation e.g. bean bags, quoits
- ✧ bench for jumping along–offering a higher and narrower surface
- ✧ jumping onto, along, off, over the bench
- ✧ negotiating obstacles on the bench
- ✧ box top
- ✧ two sections of the box
- ✧ two sections of a box, a bench and hoops on the floor to complete a circuit offering different levels and pathway

Through this kind of progressive variation in the apparatus pupils should retain their interest in each activity and in skill learning. Following the jumping station ideas suggested above, pupils should be stimulated to practise, improve, vary and extend their jumping skills. Changing the apparatus design enables the pupils to experience the same activities in different contexts. This offers scope for the repetition which is essential for improving skill mastery, but with subtle changes in challenge.

Broadening movement vocabulary

Fig 3 on page 20 shows how the supporting concept of shape can be applied to actions within the five activity categories. Relating the supporting concepts to action categories offers a means of extending the potential for variety and the development of skilled movement patterns. Figs 4–7 offer further suggestions for possible

SUPPORTING CONCEPTS

	Body Parts	Direction	Pathway	Shape	Time	Level
JUMPING	Feet to feet. Feet → hands → feet. Different foot combinations: 1 → same 1 → other 2 → 2 1 → 2 2 → 1	Forwards, backwards, sideways, diagonally, turning, e.g. 1/4, 1/2, 3/4, full.	Using concrete patterns made with bean bags, skipping ropes, hoops–lines, circles, zig zags, etc. Imaginary patterns in relation to floor, apparatus. Onto, along, across, off, over, between.	Long, wide, twisted, tucked. (Straight, tucked, star, piked, straddle.)	Fast, slow, rebound, rhythmic, big jumps, small jumps accelerating, decelerating, rhythmic variations.	Safe landing technique on floor. Take off/time in the air landing emphasis. From low apparatus, increasing the height of apparatus.
ROLLING	Trunk, fronts, sides, backs. Use of hands and legs to assist rolling. Successive contact between body parts and floor/apparatus.	Sideways, forwards, backwards, circle, diagonal. Rolls with change of direction, e.g. 1/4 turn.	In interesting apparatus circuits. Exploring pathways with linked rolls–sequence. Onto, along, off, over, between.	Long, tucked, wide. Combinations. Emphasis on shape at start during and/or end of roll.	Need to master roll with safe control before being challenged to change speed in or between rolling actions.	Floor. Inclined apparatus. Higher and/or narrower apparatus. Rolling from apparatus to floor, e.g. from kneeling on box top. Rolling up onto apparatus, e.g. from floor onto box top.

CATEGORIES

ACTIVITY						
HANGING SWINGING CLIMBING	Upper body suspending weight. Combination of hands and feet. Use of legs.	Exploring three dimensions—up/down, side/side, forwards/backwards.	Dependent on type of apparatus. Could set specific pathway challenges as feasible. Over, under, through, around.	Long, wide, tucked, twisted. Symmetrical, asymmetrical. Changing shapes during actions.	Variations should only be introduced if pupils are fully confident in negotiating the complex apparatus often used in this category.	Exploration of a range of heights and spaces. Moving up, over and down, apparatus can be emphasised as appropriate.
BALANCING	Range of body parts, e.g. hands/feet/knees/hips/shoulders/head. Large 'patches', small 'points'. Combinations.	Moving into and out of balances in different directions.	Pathway can be considered when moving into/out of balances, and when balances are integrated into sequences.	Long, tucked, wide, twisted. Symmetrical, asymmetrical. Changing shape during the balance.	Balance-challenging positions of stillness. Change speed into and out of balances.	Most balances can be mastered on the floor then challenged on higher and narrower apparatus. Some balances are easier on apparatus.
TAKING WEIGHT ON HANDS	Upper body supporting weight, body inverted partially or wholly, hips moving higher.	Hands and feet activities that move forwards, backwards, sideways, diagonally, turning.	Using concrete or imaginary pathways for exploring, zig zags, spirals, etc., on floor, and on apparatus. Onto, along, over, under, around.	Inverted shapes, long, wide, twisted, tucked. Shape changes within a skill. Symmetry, asymmetry.	Changing speed within activities should be introduced as pupils become sufficiently skilful with the basic actions.	Apparatus offering changes of level, through inclined or staged height increase, can be most useful in the early development of weight-on-hands confidence. Later more complex skills can be challenged by increasing heights and decreasing widths of apparatus.

Fig 9 Application of supporting concepts to activity categories

movement responses when pupils are challenged to consider a specific supporting concept in relation to a specific activity category.

Teachers are encouraged to use the grid, Fig 9, to extend their ideas for broadening and developing movement vocabulary. It might be useful to let the children complete, or expand their own grid. Once completed the grid can be used to show new relationships between movements. For instance, if the teacher reads one column of the grid vertically downwards, for example 'use of body parts', it is easy to recognise how different parts of the body are exercised within all five action categories. If the teacher reads a column horizontally, for example 'balancing', the diversity of material possible within one activity category can be realised.

As pupils mature and their capacity to grasp movement concepts increases, their understanding of movement potential will develop. Constant experience of the full range of gymnastic activities, combined with the application of supporting concepts will offer new perspectives and challenges. Task complexity can be gradually increased to facilitate this development. Supporting concepts can be phased into action tasks to increase the challenge, for example:

Show me changes of body shape in your rolling actions.
Show me two rolling actions which have different body shapes and a change of speed.

More detailed suggestions for developing sequence work and compositional understanding can be found in Chapter 5.

Refining movement patterns

Figs 10–25 illustrate this section, giving suggestions for possible progressions, supports and technical points all of which improve the learning of skills.

Within the illustrations some common skills within each activity category are identified as reference points for teachers developing and refining pupils' work. The families of skills thus identified are not intended as an exclusive list of skills that must be mastered. They show the common, related skills that provide examples for specific skill development within each activity category, when and where appropriate.

The skills have been selected because they are suitable for, and are frequently attempted by, primary children. It is therefore hoped their inclusion will offer teachers a useful resource. The illustrations show progression from simple to difficult stages, and technical points for safe, efficient learning.

Sample skills from families of skills within each action category have been included as follows:

Figs 10–13 on pages 35 and 36 show balancing skills, including V-sit, shoulder balance, balance on one leg and headstand.

legs straight
and together

head up

back straight
arms used to help balance

Fig 10   Balancing skills: the 'V' sit

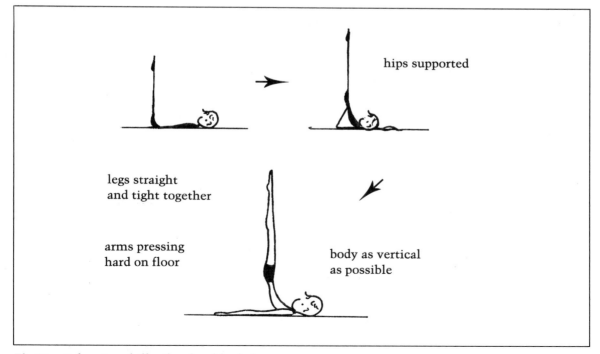

hips supported

legs straight
and tight together

arms pressing
hard on floor

body as vertical
as possible

Fig 11   Balancing skills: the shoulder balance

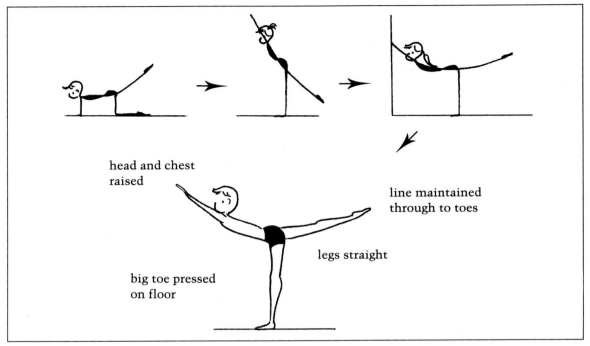

Fig 12   Balancing skills: the balance on one leg

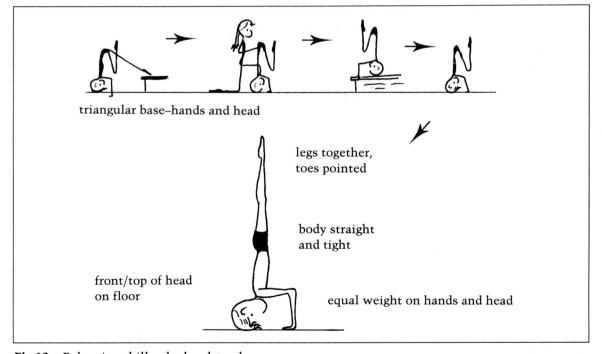

Fig 13   Balancing skills: the headstand

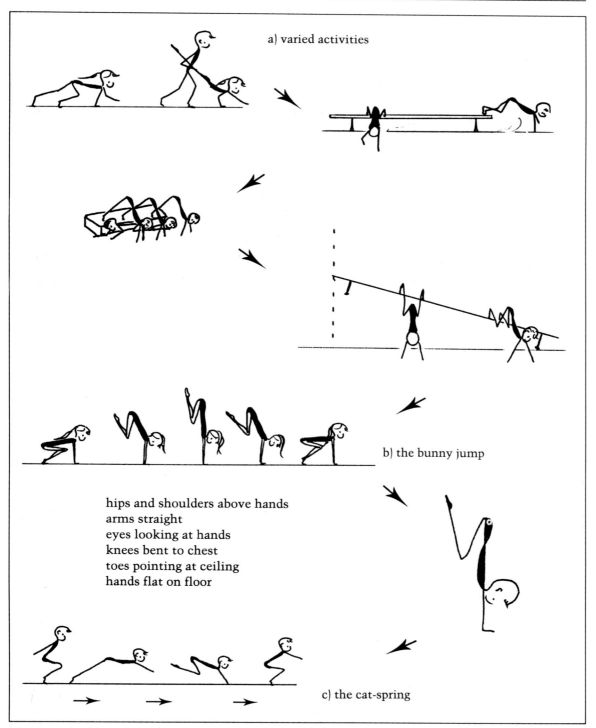

a) varied activities

b) the bunny jump

hips and shoulders above hands
arms straight
eyes looking at hands
knees bent to chest
toes pointing at ceiling
hands flat on floor

c) the cat-spring

Fig 14   Weight-on-hands: a) varied activities b) the bunny jump c) the cat-spring

climbing into handstand

kicking into handstand against a wall

support at
the hips

stepping	body	arms	eyes looking
into	straight	straight	at hands
handstand	and tight		

Fig 15   Weight-on-hands: the handstand

establishing correct co-ordinated movement pattern

gradually increasing height of hips
transfer hands to floor

support at the hips

finish stretched
in star shape

legs wide
and straight

strong push
from 'step in'
leg

start facing
forwards

Fig 16 Weight-on-hands: the cartwheel

a)

land moving through balls of feet
bend at ankles, knees and hips to absorb energy
land as quietly as possible
avoid 'deep landings' (excessive bending of knees can
injure the joint)

b)

extend body
fully without
arching back

strong upwards
swing of arms

head still,
eyes forward

prepare

strong drive with
legs and feet

Fig 17   Jumping skills: a) the landing b) the take-off

c) practising required shape

d) practising landing with feet apart first

e) always land on two feet when jumping from a height

f) in half-turn jump keep head upright
do not lean too far on take-off

Note: all jumps with changes of shape are easier if done from a little height, for example a bench. However, landings should be taught and practised before attempting to learn variations

c) the tuck jump d) the star jump e) asymmetric shape f) changing direction and turning

Figs 14–16 on pages 37 to 39 show weight-on-hands activities including the bunny jump, catspring, handstand and cartwheel.

Figs 17 a)–f) on pages 40 to 41 show correct technique, progressions and some variations for jumping skills.

Figs 18–21 on pages 43 to 45 show rolling including the log roll, circle roll, forward and backward rolls.

Figs 22–25 on pages 46 to 49 show hanging, swinging, climbing skills including hanging shapes, simple bar skills and rope climbing technique.

Gymnastics through the primary years should offer children an opportunity to master increasingly refined skilled movement patterns. The classification of activity categories offers a context within which families of skills can be safely nurtured and developed. Children will find original and skilful movement patterns within each category, particularly through the phased introduction of supporting concepts. Since they will also want to master specifically recognised gymnastic skills the teacher needs to be aware of the technical requirements and progressions which will facilitate learning.

There will be times when teachers will need to intervene with specific skill information. Some children need such help at a very early age, others much later. Teachers will make their own judgements on such matters in relation to what they have observed of the children's performance. If the majority of a class is familiar with, but not proficient at, the forward roll, the teacher might choose to spend the opening part of a lesson on break-down stages to help everyone improve this skill. Alternatively, one five-year-old might need some help on the rolling station, ahead of the rest of the class. In this case some individual help would be appropriate. The teacher is constantly faced with dilemmas over individual and whole class needs. Within every lesson the teacher will need to address both.

Aesthetic considerations

It is important to recognise that aesthetic considerations are central to and inseparable from gymnastics. In sports such as football the principal purpose of the activity, scoring a goal, is not related to the aesthetic manner of achieving it. By contrast, the purpose of the various activities in gymnastics cannot be separated from the aesthetic manner of achieving them. High technical skill should not be pursued at the expense of the aesthetic quality of the movement. The emphasis should be on the high quality of performance regardless of how simple or complex the skill. Doing one skill well before moving on to the next stage is the best advice for the safe development of skill complexity.

Developing children's awareness of the aesthetic nature of gymnastics means looking for high quality work at all times. This can be emphasised through doing and through seeing the work of others. The teacher can constantly focus attention on qualities such as: holding good starting and finishing positions, finding the right co-ordination to demonstrate control and energy efficiency, showing precision of timing and clarity of shape and line. The teacher has a vital role in helping pupils to understand and experience the aesthetic nature of gymnastics. Through teaching points, encouraging pupil observation and discussion, and ensuring correct technical knowledge, teachers will help pupils to develop such understanding. Thus, the central importance of performance within the National Curriculum for physical education cannot be seen in isolation from the evaluation/appreciation skills which are so vital in the gymnastics context.

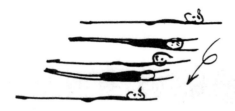

feet tight together
legs straight

Fig 18 Rolling skills: the log roll

start in   move sideways   keep pike at hips–   make a half-turn
straddle sit   first, not   hold the shape   to finish facing
position   backwards   opposite way

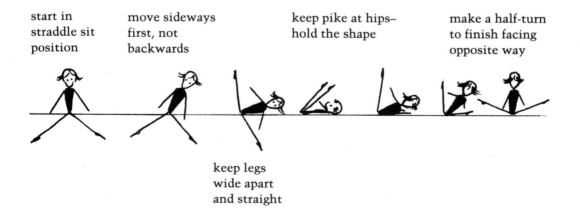

keep legs
wide apart
and straight

Fig 19 Rolling skills: the circle roll

rock backwards and forwards
in a tucked shape
chin tucked in on chest
heels close to seat

get into the roll the easy way

head tucked well in
chin on chest

rolling down a slope makes it easier to
gain the feet at the end

GOOD TECHNIQUE

| crouch down | head tucked well in, chin on chest | strong push from legs | body stays round in tight tuck shape | heels meet floor close to seat | reach well forward |

Fig 20   Rolling skills: the forward roll

toes, elbows and seat point to ceiling
hands flat on floor, under shoulders,
thumbs nearest ears

gravity helps when rolling down a
slope

support at the hips
and lift as gymnast
pushes on hands

GOOD TECHNIQUE

back rounded,
chin on chest

put feet
down first

sit, seat close to
heels, hands ready

hands flat on
floor, thumbs
nearest ears

strong push
from arms

Fig 21 Rolling skills: the backward roll

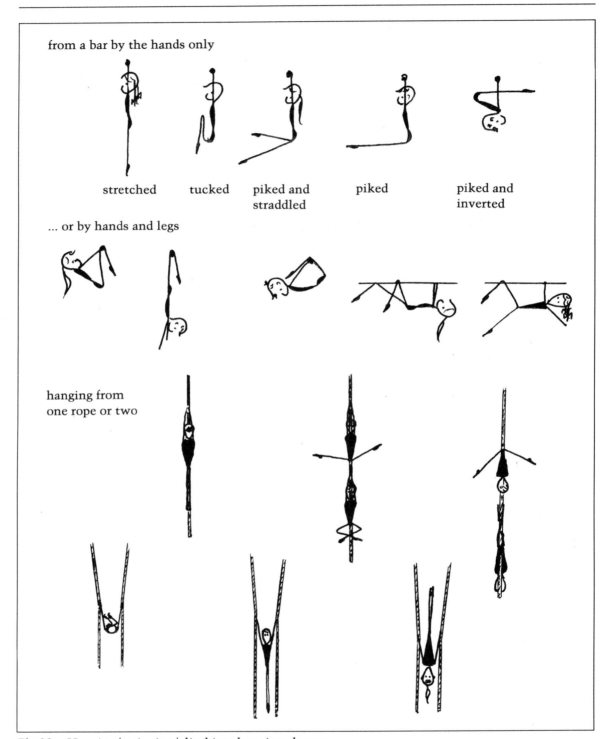

from a bar by the hands only

stretched　　tucked　　piked and　　piked　　piked and
　　　　　　　　　　　　straddled　　　　　　inverted

... or by hands and legs

hanging from
one rope or two

Fig 22　Hanging/swinging/climbing: hanging shapes

BASIC SWINGING

stretch out

kick

hips leading
under bar

press
on bar

release to
land at end
of back swing

SWING AND HALF TURN

kick

turn at end
of swing before...

swinging back

LEG ACTING UPSTART

straight leg

arms
straight

press
hips
forward

swing leg
down and
behind bar

finish
in 'mill'
support

Fig 23   Hanging/swinging/climbing: swinging skills

easy... kick over from a support

kick over bar

foot up on a support

strong pull

more difficult...   kick over from feet on floor

even more difficult...   feet together and legs straight

front support position

strong push down from shoulders

arms straight body straight and tight

FORWARD CIRCLE DOWN

lower legs and body slowly

allow legs to slide down bar

drop shoulders forward

lift heels

Fig 24   Hanging/swinging/climbing: the upward circle

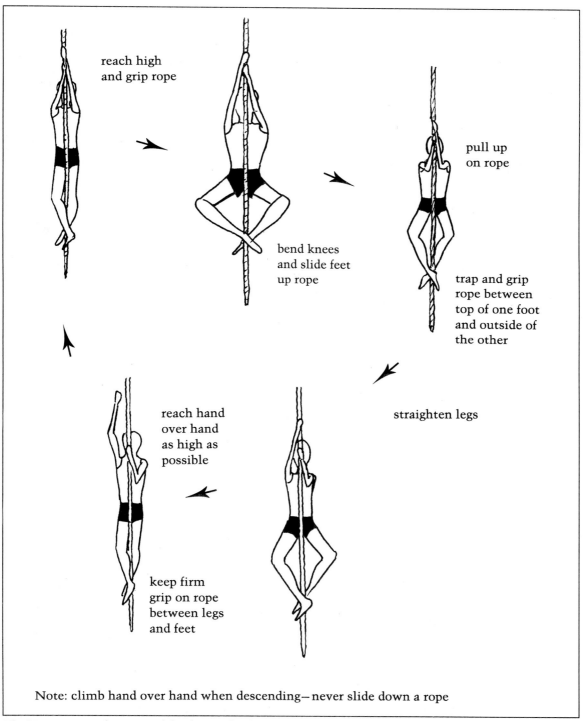

reach high
and grip rope

bend knees
and slide feet
up rope

pull up
on rope

trap and grip
rope between
top of one foot
and outside of
the other

straighten legs

reach hand
over hand
as high as
possible

keep firm
grip on rope
between legs
and feet

Note: climb hand over hand when descending – never slide down a rope

Fig 25   Hanging/swinging/climbing: climbing a rope

Five

Developing planning/composition skills

The development of planning/composition skills for sequence work in gymnastics can start in the early years and reach a high level of complexity by the top junior years. A number of stages can be identified to help teachers guide pupils in this area but individuals will progress at their own rates. This chapter offers progressive suggestions to assist in the development of knowledge and skills related to this area.

When discussing sequence work the terms 'planning' and 'composition' are used synonymously to help teachers in their application of National Curriculum requirements. However 'composition' probably offers the most appropriate term since the potential for aesthetic considerations in complex gymnastic sequence development goes beyond 'planning'.

Developing a basic movement vocabulary

Initially children will need to develop a vocabulary of gymnastic movements. Regular exposure to floor and apparatus work related to the five activity categories of the multi-activities approach, will encourage such development. Strategies such as sharing ideas through demonstrations, teacher suggestion and pupil exploration will help to broaden awareness and competence with varied movement patterns.

Where required the teacher needs to feed in technical knowledge to help children achieve success in their movement actions. They may need help with preparing for an action, the action itself or recovering from the action. For example, children should be aware of the importance of preparation and landing in jumping, of a round body shape with chin tucked in onto chest for forward rolling, of concentrating when moving into a balance position and how to move out of that balance position. The level of technical help required depends on the age and ability of the child. The teacher's role is to observe and respond to pupils' needs.

There will be occasions when some intervention is essential to ensure greater safety and success. Regular experience of movement patterns related to jumping, balancing, rolling, taking weight-on-hands and hanging/swinging/climbing will offer a sound basis for developing sequence work or the linking of different movement patterns into phrases.

Linking like movement patterns

Once children can differentiate types of movements and can perform some skills safely within each activity category the teacher can introduce the idea of sequencing movements. Like movement patterns can be used first, for example a series of rolls down the mattress, or a series of hops around a circle of hoops, as in Fig 26. Without any set number to consider pupils can concentrate on the linking aspect. The most difficult part of any sequence work is the transition between elements. At this stage it is helpful to emphasise the continuity of movements with the end of one action leading straight into the next.

Once pupils have the idea of a series of movements which flow together they can cope with boundaries to that series, for example three rolls down the mattress or six hops around the circle of hoops. Fig 27 shows two log rolls. Clearly this stage can be useful in reinforcing the development of number concepts. The vital importance of good starting and finishing awareness can be introduced very early on, for example:

Show me how you are going to start.

Hold your finishing position.

This illustrates the importance of good form and will set excellent foundations for future development. As well as

Fig 26 Hopping round a circle of hoops

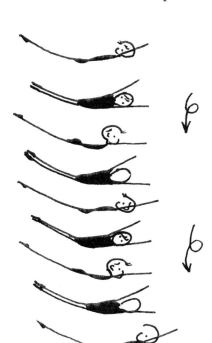

Fig 27 Two log rolls

responding to directed tasks such as those suggested, pupils should also be encouraged to choose their own movement responses within less directed tasks, for example:

Choose your favourite jumping action and show me three in a row.

Linking different movements within an action category

Sequencing different movements from within one activity category can present a more challenging task. Having built up a range of balancing skills pupils could be asked to choose two different balances and put them into a sequence. They will need help on moving skilfully into and out of the balances if the finished sequence is to have continuity. Fig 28 shows a possible sequence of balances, and Fig 29 a sequence of jumps. This reinforces the need for good teaching during early movement explorations so that preparation, action and recovery are mastered in the development of controlled movement patterns. The task complexity can be developed by increasing the number of actions linked in the sequence.

Fig 28   A sequence of balances

Fig 29   A sequence of jumps

Linking movements across action categories

Linking like movement patterns, that is those within activity categories, can be followed by linking movements from across categories. Pupils might find it helpful to have a definite directed combination at first, starting with two actions, for example a star jump and a bunny jump (from the jumping and weight-on-hands categories). The transition point of absorbing the landing of the jump into the crouch position for the bunny jump needs stressing so that continuity is achieved. This presupposes all children have the ability to achieve success with the skills selected.

Subsequent wider tasks would encourage pupil choice, for example:

Join your favourite balance and your favourite roll to make a sequence.

Teachers need to remember that some combinations are physically much more difficult than others. To perform a dynamic jumping action into a static balance involves a high level of control, whereas to hold a balance like an arabesque and tip into a roll is not as difficult. The complexity can be increased by extending the number and diversity of actions in the sequence. Here are some examples with progressive levels of complexity:

Can you make up a sequence which has two jumps and two weight-on-hands actions?

Make up a sequence which has one jump, one roll and one balance.

Make up a sequence which has three jumps, one balance and two rolls.

Fig 30 shows a sequence of actions from different categories.

Applying supporting concepts to sequences

When the pupils have sufficient competence with differentiated movement patterns and an understanding of the concept of sequence, they can develop and extend their skills and sequence abilities by considering the supporting movement concepts in relation to the five basic movement categories.

Fig 30   A sequence of actions from different categories

Initially they will need to explore concepts like shape, direction, speed and body parts in relation to each movement category, for example:

As you climb on the frame today show me how many different directions you can use.

Can you move into your balance backwards or sideways?

This will extend pupils' thinking and their movement vocabulary. With these additional movement possibilities pupils can further extend their sequence work. Evidence of pupils' ability to apply these concepts can be assessed through their response to related sequence tasks, for example:

Show me a sequence of three jumps which move into three different directions.

Can you join together three balances on three different parts of the body? (See Fig 31.)

Complexity can be further increased by adding to the number of different action and supporting concept variables to be considered:

Can you make up a sequence of balances which shows change of level and use of different body parts?

Build a sequence using a jump, a roll and a weight-on-hands action, which has clear changes of speed and direction.

The variables and potential challenge are infinite.

Partner-work in sequences

When the time is appropriate for the pupils the idea of partner-work can be introduced to extend the interest and scope of gymnastic sequence development. Pupils must have some desire to co-operate with others and some sense of responsibility to ensure the gymnastics lesson retains the necessary controlled and well-disciplined environment essential for safety.

Initially pupils can experiment with simple matching, or follow-the-leader ideas, working in unison with a partner, and working in canon. They can try a range of actions and perhaps some simple sequence construction to explore and develop these ideas further, along with other partner-work ideas.

Fig 31   Three balances on three different parts of the body

See Photos 4–6 on page 56 for examples of some partner-work concepts: mirroring, using partner as obstacle counter-balancing.

Working with such ideas the children will gradually gain the sensitivity required to co-operate with others. At more advanced stages these ideas can be extended to working in larger groups. This type of work offers new challenges and rewards.

The teacher may use partner-work for a variety of reasons. For example a short directed sequence, within everyone's capabilities, may be set to see if pairs can persevere for accuracy in matched timing. An open-ended task may be used to allow children to negotiate content, practise and refine ideas. More working time will be needed for partner tasks due to the number of decisions, social skills and practical adaptations required.

There may be a time when the children will respond positively to the idea of supporting a partner in the safe learning of skills such as a headstand or handstand. The class teacher, with his or her detailed knowledge of the children and their potential, is the best judge of when and how such supporting skills might be appropriately introduced.

Working in groups

If pupils reach a high level of achievement in partner sequence work they might enjoy the different challenge offered by working in small groups. There is much to discover, for example about the compositional possibilities of working in an odd numbered group of three, in comparison with an even numbered group of four, or the patterning possibilities of group work.

Sequences using apparatus

The examples used in this section have largely related to floor-work but once basic movement confidence has been mastered apparatus sequences can parallel floor sequence work. An example of an apparatus sequence can be seen in Fig 32 on page 57.

If children are going to link movements together on apparatus clearly they must be able to negotiate the range of apparatus available, show the self-discipline to share apparatus sensibly, and be able to control movements onto, along and off apparatus. If partner-work is to be developed on apparatus the lay-out must reflect possibilities, for example matching and mirroring tasks would need opportunities like parallel or opposite benches at a station, as shown in Fig 2, page 14.

Using music in sequences

Finally, music can add another dimension to gymnastic composition. Music can be introduced in a variety of ways. The younger pupils might enjoy moving to music in warm-ups, which can be motivating and stimulating. Gradually children can be

4 Mirroring

5 Using partner as an obstacle

6 Counter-balancing

Fig 32   Example of an apparatus sequence

encouraged to listen and move with the phrasing of the music, through a combination of warm-up activities or a set of short actions that fit with the musical phrasing. As a regular feature of gymnastic lessons pupils can be introduced to a range of musical rhythms and dynamics which will add interest and variety to performance and musical knowledge.

Older children might enjoy composing a sequence to music. The challenge of using music in composing a floor, apparatus, individual, partner or small group gymnastic sequence can be highly complex if movement phrasing is to complement musical phrasing. With a consistent, progressive gymnastic programme top junior children are capable of achieving considerable success in this area. The teacher could set task parameters to the content, as suggested above, or allow the pupils to construct their own tasks, choose their own music and/or design their own apparatus. Pupils will enjoy sharing these responsibilities. The variables are innumerable. The more complex the task the more time is required to fulfil the challenge. Use of video recording and playback can be an interesting learning medium if available.

As sequences reach this level of sophistication pupils can be asked to consider a range of supporting concepts that will enhance the gymnastics skills being amalgamated, for example use of floor pattern, rhythmic content and use of different directions. These concepts will have been introduced in earlier years but can now be revisited at a higher level of complexity. Even at this stage it must be remembered that the core action content in these gymnastic sequences will be skilful movement patterns developed within the five activity categories. These always remain at the centre of this multi-activities approach. The supporting concepts remain just that, means by which gymnastic actions are extended and varied, ensuring infinite scope for development.

Progressive task complexity

What follows are suggestions for making sequencing tasks increasingly complex:

1 *Can you show me jumping on the spot?*
2 *Show me three hops.*
3 *Join together a shoulder balance and a knee balance.*
4 *Choose two different balances and join them in a sequence.*
5 *Make up a sequence using your favourite jump and roll.*
6 *Can you show me a sequence which has one balance, one roll and one jump?*
7 *In your rolling sequence I would like you to introduce a clear change of speed.*
8 *Can you make a zig-zag pathway on the climbing frame? Where does your pattern start and finish?*
9 *Choose three weight-on-hands actions with three different shapes and join them together in a sequence.*
10 *Link an explosive jump with a slow forward roll finishing in a balance of your choice.*
11 *Using taking weight-on-hands, rolling and balancing make up a sequence that shows three changes of body shape and movements into three different directions.*
12 *With your partner make up a rolling sequence which shows matching and/or mirroring.*
13 *Using this music construct a partner sequence to show contact and non-contact work. You have a free choice on action content.*
14 *Using jumping, rolling and balancing make up a sequence that uses all the apparatus at your station and shows four different ways of working with your partner.*
15 *Over the next three weeks you are going to create a sequence, with a partner, making all the decisions for*

yourselves. You have to agree on a piece of music for the class to use. You must write out the sequence task you set so you can evaluate each other's sequences when they are finished. You need to decide:
- *will it be a floor or apparatus sequence?*
- *which mat pattern or apparatus do you want?*
- *which skills or action categories will you include?*
- *which supporting ideas like shape or direction will you use?*
- *which relationship ideas like matching or follow-the-leader will you show?'*

On page 60 there is a diagrammatic summary of the potential for sequence development outlined in this chapter.

SUMMARY OF PROGRESSION IN GYMNASTIC COMPOSITION

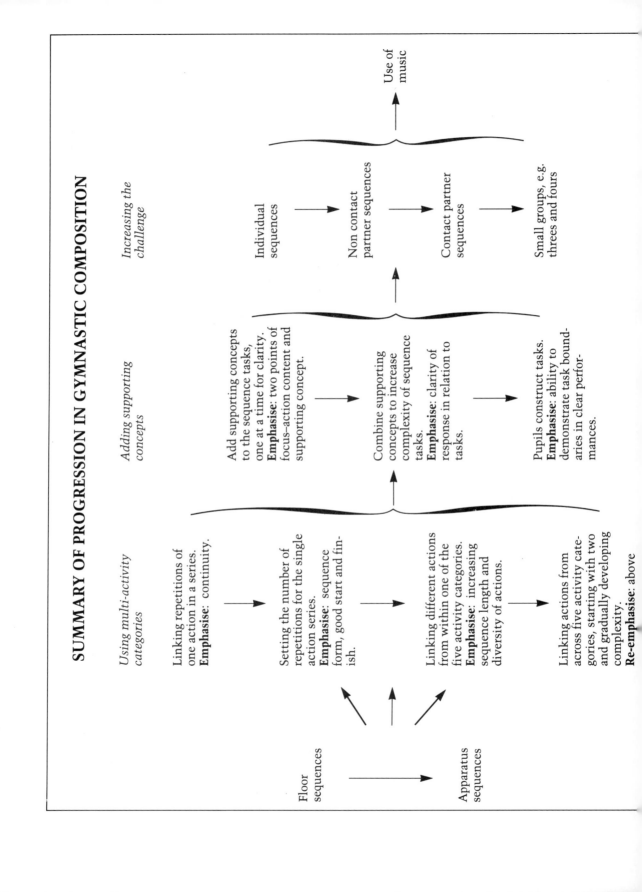

Using multi-activity categories

Adding supporting concepts

Increasing the challenge

Linking repetitions of one action in a series. **Emphasise:** continuity.

Setting the number of repetitions for the single action series. **Emphasise:** sequence form, good start and finish.

Linking different actions from within one of the five activity categories. **Emphasise:** increasing sequence length and diversity of actions.

Linking actions from across five activity categories, starting with two and gradually developing complexity. **Re-emphasise:** above

Add supporting concepts to the sequence tasks, one at a time for clarity. **Emphasise:** two points of focus–action content and supporting concept.

Combine supporting concepts to increase complexity of sequence tasks. **Emphasise:** clarity of response in relation to tasks.

Pupils construct tasks. **Emphasise:** ability to demonstrate task boundaries in clear performances.

Individual sequences

Non contact partner sequences

Contact partner sequences

Small groups, e.g. threes and fours

Use of music

Floor sequences

Apparatus sequences

Six

Developing evaluation/appreciation skills

Aesthetic quality is a central characteristic of gymnastic movement. Indeed, the aesthetic aspect of movement is inseparable from the character of the activity. Thus gymnastics can provide one of the most fruitful vehicles for developing children's aesthetic appreciation of human movement.

The National Curriculum has highlighted the fact that good physical education teaching should provide opportunities for developing evaluation skills. In order to help teachers with the National Curriculum the terms 'evaluation' and 'appreciation' are used synonymously to refer to that area of skill-learning related to perceptions of quality, value and judgement. However, the essentially aesthetic nature of gymnastics makes 'appreciation' a more appropriate description of potential skill-learning than 'evaluation'. This is because increasingly knowledgeable perceptions of aesthetic qualities can be achieved through this context.

In gymnastics aesthetic qualities such as shape, form, line, pattern, skills, continuity and the harmonious linking of movements are fundamentally important. Performance, composition and appreciation skills in gymnastics must therefore involve the understanding of aesthetic values of human movement.

It is often the case, in other contexts of physical education, that the aesthetic aspects of how a movement is performed is not the ultimate concern for the teacher or the learner. For example, in some games scoring the goals might be of greater importance than how the goals were scored. In swimming, moving with feet off the bottom across a width might be more important, at a particular time, than the quality of the movements used. Technical idiosyncrasies in athletic performances sometimes appear in the production of a higher jump or a faster sprint. Such idiosyncrasies might not be aesthetic to watch but might be acceptable on the grounds of serving other, more important, purposes.

This is not to suggest that aspects of the aesthetic are not available through all physical education contexts. Rather it is to reinforce the contention that in gymnastics concern for aesthetic qualities can never be separated from achievement, and therefore must have considerable emphasis in teaching and learning. These issues have been extensively argued elsewhere, for example in the 'aesthetic sports'/'purposive sports' distinction made by Professor David Best (9).

Improving the appreciation of movement should be encouraged in every gymnastics lesson. Pupils can be constantly involved in such processes as observing, discussing, making constructive comments on their own work and that of others, and making informed value-judgements on the quality of movement experiences. Teachers will find their own ways of engaging children in such processes. The ideas presented in this chapter are offered as a guide to developing the skills of evaluation or appreciation in the gymnastics context, and in relation to the multi-activities approach.

Teacher observation

Using the multi-activities approach, with the five activity categories, the teacher could assess the pupils' understanding by observing movement responses to action tasks. For example, pupils' ability to differentiate between the major action categories is easily recognised in movement responses specifically related to jumping, or rolling or balancing tasks.

Pupil description of observations

Teachers could encourage pupils to respond verbally to questions about what they observe of other children at work. Pupils who are able to identify and describe the different basic activities would be developing language skills in relation to their physical and observational skills.

Emphasis on quality of movement

This can be introduced from the earliest lessons. It can be achieved through the teacher making appropriate technical demands of the children, with comments such as:

Quiet landings from jumps, bending the knees.

During later observation the pupils might be asked to use this knowledge critically. For example, the teacher might say:

Let's watch the jumping group. Are they all jumping well? Can we help them to improve their jumping?

Development of movement vocabulary

Once pupils can differentiate actions in the five activity categories, more specific awareness of movement vocabulary, within each category, may begin to be developed. For example, hopping, galloping, skipping and leaping are all different actions within the category of jumping. Pupils need to be encouraged to develop and extend their language skills and vocabulary alongside their movement skills and movement vocabulary. This is achieved, in good practice, through ensuring that children are involved in the learning processes of doing, seeing and discussing as they progress through their primary years.

For example the teacher might say:

Watch the jumping station and see if you can name three different ways of jumping.

Look at the different balances performed by the group. Can you name the balances? Which was the hardest balance? Why do you think it was the most difficult?

The last question demands a much more complex response than the others, involving recall, understanding and movement analysis.

Critical awareness of technique

As actions become more refined into specific skills children will be learning points of technique enabling more efficient performance. They will also be increasing their understanding of safety in relation to skilful performance, such as how and why they would need to support at the hips if helping a partner to do a handstand. At all stages children should be encouraged to reinforce their learning through:

⋄ critical discussion
⋄ the application of their knowledge and understanding to questions
⋄ when appropriate, reciprocal teaching opportunities

Such opportunities would require analysis, application of knowledge and communication skills.

Consider an example from the development of a handstand skill. This might be developed within the family of skills related to the weight-on-hands activity category (see Chapter 4).

The teacher might ask:

Is this a good handstand? Why?

Can anyone tell me how we could help John to make his handstand straighter? Is there an exercise we could suggest to help him with leg tension? (See Chapter 11 on body preparation.)

Movement analysis using supporting concepts

In a well-planned school policy (see Chapter 7) the phased introduction of supporting movement concepts, such as body shape, direction and use of body parts, adds increased complexity to performance within the five activity categories. The principles also offer increased complexity for movement observation and analysis skills. The following examples illustrate a range of movement analysis questions which the teacher might ask using the supporting concepts:

In this jump, roll and balance sequence how does Sarah show three changes of body shape?

How many assymmetric shapes are there in Fasad's sequence?
Can you make a record of the actions, shape-changes and direction-changes your partner has used in his or her sequence?

Pupil observation of sequences

Important sequence development features can be reinforced by focusing pupils' attention during observation tasks. For example, qualities such as a clear start, fluent linking of movements, and a clear finish are all identifiable features. Observation and performance tasks become more complex in parallel. For example, checking for actions, changes of speed and direction might necessitate three viewings by an observing partner.

The task becomes more complex as the pupils are encouraged to offer suggestions for improving the sequences of others, for example helping to re-order movements for a more fluent sequence, or suggesting minor changes to clarify the response to the task. This not only requires considered understanding of movement analysis, but skills of communication, such as criticising constructively and negotiating improvements that will result in work of higher quality and greater value, both to the performer and to the observer.

Pupil observation of originality

Teachers might direct observational skills towards efforts for originality. Having identified an unusual response to a task the teacher might ask:

How does Sunita's balancing on apparatus differ from everyone else's?

Look at David's start to his sequence, why is it unusual?

This gives value to original responses by drawing attention to them, and encouraging analysis of that originality.

There are many other aspects of gymnastics which can benefit from, and contribute to, skills of evaluation/appreciation. One of these is the critical observation of a range of relationship concepts such as matching and mirroring in partner and group work situations. Other challenges, such as matching the phrasing of music when creating gymnastic sequences can also extend the learning potential of the gymnastics context.

Evaluation/appreciation skills should develop alongside performance and planning/ composition skills. For instance, where lessons are focused on children improving their performance skills, learning can be reinforced and extended by encouraging pupils to become actively involved in observation, questioning and discussion. Equally, critical application of knowledge and understanding can be developed when the emphasis is on composition or sequence work.

The examples suggested in this chapter so far are intended to provide ideas of progression in learning. As children move through the primary years they first acquire simple skills of observation, like identifying, recognising and describing movements. Subsequently they move on to develop the more complex skills of movement appreciation. These will include the analysis of factors contributing to skilful movement, applying knowledge critically to their own work and the work of others, and recognising and facilitating work of high quality through constructive critical interaction with each other.

Examples of progressive learning

Attention to this aspect of learning within the teaching process should enable children to:

- ◇ demonstrate understanding of different movement types, for example by performing jumps, balances, rolls
- ◇ recognise and describe differentiated movement patterns
- ◇ comment constructively on their own movement patterns and/or those of others
- ◇ identify criteria of good technique, for example 'quiet landings on jumps'—this can build from simple action analysis to complex skill analysis
- ◇ verbalise a broadening movement vocabulary related to actions, for example identifying hopping, galloping, skipping, leaping within the 'jumping' family of skills
- ◇ identify and discuss the application of supporting concepts, for example changing body shape or direction of movement, to developing variety and interest in movement patterns
- ◇ describe different relationship concepts, for example matching, mirroring, working in unison or canon, and suggest improvements
- ◇ observe, remember and possibly record, sequences of increasing complexity, for example action content, supporting concept content, relationship content if partner or small group sequence
- ◇ recognise aesthetic qualities that contribute to good performance, for example continuity and form in sequence work, line and amplitude of movement in specific skills
- ◇ evaluate their own performances and those of others in relation to given criteria
- ◇ communicate critical judgements sensitively and constructively
- ◇ select their own criteria for making value-judgements on their own work and that of others
- ◇ participate in sharing responsibility for assessment of their own work and that of others

Managing opportunities for observation

Children's appreciation skills, such as analysing, understanding and reflecting on movement, can be improved if opportunities are fostered by the teachers. Such opportunities can be built in from the first lesson in a variety of ways. Every lesson should include some aspect of 'looking', since, as previously explained, appreciation skills develop in parallel with performance and composition skills. Some examples of ways in which this can be done are:

1 At the end of the lesson the children could show the teacher their 'best final attempt'. Even at this level the emphasis in gymnastics can be on quality of work, and is worthy of a response from the teacher which goes beyond the simple 'good'.

2 Half the class could observe the work of the other half, in turn. Pupils need a focus for their observations. For instance, they may be directed to look for a specific action or point of technique in the demonstration. It is important that every demonstration is followed up by involving the observers in responding. The level of response the teacher will encourage is dependent on the experience of the children.

3 With the children in pairs, numbered one and two, number ones can show their work to number twos, and vice versa. The children should have a substantial opportunity to discuss aspects of the work exchanged.

4 The teacher could select one pupil to demonstrate a particular movement pattern. Other children need to be able to see the demonstrator clearly, and understand what they are looking for in the work they are observing. After the demonstration they will interact with the teacher and each other in discussing, analysing, or responding in other ways to the purpose of the demonstration, such as recording. Where appropriate this should be followed with pupils applying the points they have learnt to improving their own work.

5 When the children are at the stage where they recognise and enjoy the need to practise and repeat movement patterns in order to improve the skill level, then some sharing on a larger scale can be valuable. In this kind of sharing experience the performing/viewing roles suggested above are extended to the preparation of work which is specifically intended for viewing by others. There is little doubt that having an event to focus on can result in increased qualities of perseverance, effort and achievement in pupils. As well as developing a higher skill level, a shared performance often adds to a child's self-confidence and feeling of worth. Seeing and participating in such gymnastic events can also help children to develop a

broader understanding from which to evaluate gymnastics work, their own and that of others. Ways in which such experiences can be fostered are:

Inter-class sharing

Inter-class sharing of gymnastics work provides an opportunity for children to develop a piece of work which is intended to be shared with other classes within the year-group or school. Other children reciprocate the experience by watching and performing their specially prepared work in turn. The teachers need to be clear about why they are sharing work, and precisely what the children are going to learn from the experience.

Inter-school sharing

Inter-school sharing experiences, for example local festivals of gymnastics, can also be valuable opportunities for learning. These can be easily organised between local schools. A date and central venue are set. Children prepare gymnastics work of a prescribed length and perform it on the festival day. The purpose is to enhance the profile of gymnastics through public awareness, and to provide an opportunity for children to exhibit their work.

Wider festivals of gymnastics

There may be locally held festivals of gymnastics which facilitate links between schools and community gymnastic clubs. These are becoming increasingly popular as the General Gymnastics branch of the British Amateur Gymnastics Association fosters and develops teacher-education and coach-education on the value of such festivals. In such an event pupils could be fortunate enough to perform with, and observe, a wide spectrum of activities. For example, there might be display items which relate to the sporting disciplines of gymnastics which are the artistic, rhythmic and sports acrobatics forms. There might also be displays by recreational classes, for adults and children, special needs gymnastic groups, and pre-school children.

In other European countries such festivals currently enjoy a high profile, often involving all members of the family, and wide media attention. Such festivals can help participants to increase their understanding and appreciation of human achievement in people of all ages and abilities.

Seven

Developing a whole-school policy

Two essential features for fruitful and progressive learning are continuity and consistency. If these are to be achieved a long-term perspective is required in the planning, teaching and evaluation of the curriculum. It is particularly important in the primary school where excessive curricular and day-to-day demands often make it difficult to ensure that work in every subject area builds upon previous foundations or progresses towards future achievement. One way in which teachers can facilitate such continuity is to participate in the preparation of a whole-school policy for each area of the curriculum. This chapter is concerned with such a policy for gymnastics.

A policy is beneficial only if its contents are adopted by the teachers in a school. In developing a school policy the curriculum leader will have a special role to play in advising and listening to colleagues. But the most effective policy will be produced from the combined collaboration of all teachers at a school. By personally initiating and contributing to the ideas and strategies of the policy each teacher will feel more personally committed to its implementation.

One particularly important decision which should be made in the formulation of a gymnastics policy is that of teaching approach. Currently there are several approaches, for example the thematic, the skills-based and the multi-activities approach described in this book. Each one is based on a different classification of movement content. Consequently each offers a different means of organising content material and structuring progressive learning experiences for pupils. It is important, therefore, to decide which approach should form the basis of the school's teaching. Staff workshops to increase awareness of alternative approaches might be necessary before an informed choice can be made.

It is desirable for each teacher to work within an approach which he or she finds most comfortable. However, young children might not understand the gymnastic continuity in a school which offers one year a thematic approach, the next skills-based and the next multi-activities. Success in any approach is dependent on having time to establish the learning and understanding that can be achieved. With far from ideal initial and in-service opportunities, it would be rare to meet a primary teacher who felt prepared or confident to work across different approaches. Consequently adopting one approach might be helpful in focusing in-service training, staff discussion and the development of a progressive school programme.

Adopting one approach should not be restrictive for teachers since the successful use of each approach mentioned is dependent on teachers' flexibility in responding to the particular needs of pupils, and to the time and resources available. A major advantage of adopting one approach would be the agreement on a conceptual basis, for example the action categories and supporting concepts that form the basis of the multi-activities approach. Such a basis would enable teachers to collaborate for planning, assessing and reviewing their work in gymnastics. This would have a positive effect on teacher confidence, and, in turn, on the teaching of gymnastics.

A common teaching approach within a school would help ensure that, as they moved through the primary years, pupils would continually meet familiar procedures and expectations. It would also facilitate sound, safe progression of learning experiences.

The multi-activities approach will be used to structure sample stages of development in learning, from reception to year six (see Chapter 8). The potential breadth and depth of the action and supporting concepts classifications, alongside the performance, planning and evaluation perspectives of learning, described in Chapters 4, 5 and 6, enable systematic progression to be built into a school policy.

The development of a whole-school policy for gymnastics teaching raises a number of considerations:

  ⋄ the parameters of the policy
  ⋄ practical decisions for the policy
  ⋄ how the gymnastic content is to be developed
  ⋄ what means of assessment/evaluation are to be adopted

The parameters of a school policy

Before an attempt is made to build progressive content into a school policy for gymnastics teaching it is essential to take account of a number of related factors. These include a corporate commitment, the level of staff knowledge and expertise as well as the time, space and equipment available.

Head teacher commitment

This issue must be addressed since commitment from the head teacher might well be essential in finding the funds for new equipment or repairs. Finance, time to provide in-service training and the necessary support for the school curriculum leader, are also vital ingredients often determined by the head teacher.

Staff commitment

If the staff decide pupils will have gymnastics on the timetable for some period in each school year, the implication is that every member of that staff will be involved in the teaching of gymnastics. There may be ways of negotiating alternatives, in unavoidable situations, but generally the class teacher has the obligation to provide the learning experience. With his or her unique perception of the total learning environment of primary children, there is little doubt that the class teacher is the best person to teach gymnastics. The proviso should be that he or she feels sufficiently confident to offer safe and progressive learning in this context. If not there may be implications for staff development needs.

Staff development

Time and resources for staff development are limited therefore it would help to maximise efficiency if the teachers could identify their greatest needs in this area. For example, is the most urgent need that of understanding the basic principles of a new approach, of designing imaginative apparatus plans, of fostering progression through appropriate tasks, or that of teaching and supporting specific skills?

Relating policy to National Curriculum

Taking into consideration their knowledge, the time and resources available, and their statutory obligation, staff will have to consider how they can offer the breadth of activity contexts required by the National Curriculum. The Non-Statutory Guidance recommends weekly lessons in games, dance and gymnastics across Key Stages One and Two. In addition schools should offer athletic activities, swimming and outdoor and adventurous activities. This means long-term planning of a school policy for physical education in relation to National Curriculum recommendations and school-based feasibility. Such planning should precede detailed gymnastics planning.

Availability of hall time

An important issue affecting the depth and breadth of the gymnastic policy is the amount of time each class can spend in the hall on gymnastics in a school year. Some children may have a lesson a week throughout their primary school years. Others might receive shorter blocked time on gymnastics to allow for some dance or time at the swimming pool. Clearly the possible development of work and levels of achievement would be different.

The availability of the primary school hall can constrain the amount of time allocated to the teaching of gymnastics. This space has to cater for a host of different demands, such as assemblies, dinners, storage space, video room, music/physical education/drama teaching space, spare classroom teaching space and performances. So each school needs to establish the indoor time that can be made available for physical education per class per term per year.

Length of lessons

It is suggested that younger children will respond eagerly and with maximum effect in short lessons, for example 25 minutes. As children mature they are more able to cope with sustained opportunities to practise, repeat, and improve their work. Therefore lesson time should be increased with pupil maturity, if possible.

Information gained from discussing the above issues will enable the school policy parameters to be identified. Clearly there will be major differences between schools on factors such as time availability and resource opportunities for physical education.

Practical decisions for a school policy

Finally, it is essential to discuss the practical issues that affect continuity of experience for pupils. For example, standardising expectations in relation to clothing, and rules about the safety and movement of apparatus, will enable class teachers to reinforce policies and procedures, rather than re-teach them every time a new school year begins.

Clothing

1 What is the policy on long hair in relation to safety? Do you insist on its being tied back?
2 What is the policy on removal of jewellery for physical education? Do you need to consider jewellery worn for religious reasons?
3 What do the children wear for gymnastics? In particular what is the policy on footwear? (For work of the highest quality in gymnastics, as in dance, the children need to work in bare feet but this is not always possible when floors are unsuitable.)

Apparatus

1 Where is the apparatus stored? Is it accessible? Could there be an agreed system of storing apparatus to enable easy access to mats, benches, planks, boxes etc? (For example, apparatus stored around the outside of the hall could be moved more

easily and therefore more safely, and would probably be used more frequently. The children would benefit from knowing where each piece of apparatus could be found and how they were expected to leave it.)

2 Do the teachers use the same names for the different pieces of apparatus? It is surprising how many differences there can be in this area.

3 Is the apparatus easily moved? Would a set of rules help with standardising how pieces are moved? Would such rules be different for infant and junior aged children? (Training children to move apparatus is part of gymnastics, but it takes time. Initially teachers might need to move much of the equipment themselves and then gradually share these responsibilities with the children. Pupils will learn how to handle the range and size of apparatus through a systematic, appropriate 'moving of apparatus' section within the policy. Such an agreed policy would enable teachers to build on clearly defined expectations. There are more ideas for the safe use of apparatus in Chapter 10.)

Safety

1 Are there ways in which staff could share responsibility for safety? For example there could be corporate responsibility for checking and reporting any problems with the apparatus or floor.

2 Would it be helpful to have guidance on safety checks by the teacher in lessons? For example checking boxes are off wheel carriages, tension wires are secured on climbing frames, landing areas safe.

3 It might be wise to discuss accident procedure to be followed should the need arise. For example, if there is an accident what should the teacher do with the rest of the class? Who is qualified in first aid in the school? Who makes arrangements for calling an ambulance if necessary? Who informs the parents? Is there an accident form which would need completing?

Record-keeping

Are there records of achievement available for informing colleagues of progress/achievement in this area for the start of each school year? How do staff currently avoid repetition and ensure continuity in pupil-learning? What form do or could records take? Do staff pass on other important information, for example, in relation to medical problems?

The questions raised need to be addressed in each school situation so that a relevant and specific policy can be agreed and developed.

Resolving such issues through discussion could save time in those first important weeks of each school year. It would also be easier for new staff and students if they could follow a school policy on such practical issues and attempt to retain normal procedures in relation to pupil and teacher expectations. Once general parameters and practical decisions are made teachers can consider progressive planning.

Suggestions for whole-school policy planning on gymnastics content and assessment follow in Chapters 8 and 9.

Eight
_____

Sample teaching programmes for Key Stages One and Two

The following examples illustrate how a programme of teaching/ learning in gymnastics across the 4–11 age range might evolve. For the reasons outlined in Chapter 7 every school must devise their own personalised school policy. The following ideas for units of work are suggestions as to how teachers might plan for pupils' progression in learning performance, planning/composition and evaluation/appreciation skills across Key Stages One and Two.

Each unit represents a half-term block of time. One unit per primary year is offered as an example of possible progression from reception to year six. The examples assume continuity of gymnastics lessons in interim terms.

Where appropriate the performance, planning/composition and evaluation/ appreciation skills relevant in each half-term block of work, are indicated. These have been abstracted from the progressions outlined in earlier chapters, to illustrate their co-existence in the holistic teaching/learning situation.

Reception and Key Stage One
Depending on nursery experience when children enter their reception year they may need to become familiar with many procedures essential to physical education. These can be integrated into early units or schemes of work as illustrated in the first example.

Unit A – Reception class

Aims
- ✧ To familiarise pupils with general changing and lesson format procedures.
- ✧ To introduce pupils to the five activity categories in the multi-activities approach on the floor and on apparatus.

Performance
Exploration of the five activity categories: balancing, jumping, rolling, taking weight-on-hands and hanging/swinging/climbing, through floor and apparatus experiences.

FLOOR-WORK
Basic introduction to one activity during floor-work time each
week.
>WEEK 1: JUMPING
>WEEK 2: ROCKING/ROLLING
>WEEK 3: BALANCING
>WEEK 4: WEIGHT-ON-HANDS

WEEKS 5–8: re-visit those activities in floor-work time to extend
understanding of the differentiated categories, basic techniques
and movement mastery. The teacher should encourage a broad
range of responses within the movement categories used.

APPARATUS
Simple apparatus circuit to encourage the five different activities
(see Fig 1 on page 12).

Evaluation/appreciation
Observation and recognition of differentiated movements within
the five categories of activity.

Unit B – Year 1

Aim
>✧ To emphasise quality of movement and variety of actions
>within each category, with particular attention to jumping
>and balancing.

Performance
FLOOR-WORK
Broadening vocabulary and improving skill level in jumping and
balancing
>WEEKS 1–4: JUMPING

Introduce vocabulary within activity categories, for example
jumping activities might include hopping, skipping, leaping,
galloping. Emphasise technique as appropriate, for example with
jumping activities emphasise landing technique, absorbing
momentum in leg muscles, bending the knees, quiet landings.
>WEEKS 5–8: BALANCING

Introduce balancing on different body parts to encourage varied
explorations. Particular emphasis can be placed on recognising
that the smaller the base the more difficult the balance becomes.

APPARATUS
Continue exploring the five movement categories on a new
apparatus lay-out. Particular attention can be placed on the
development of jumping and balancing actions on the apparatus

stations designed for these specific activities. Develop the challenge by asking for sequences of 'like' movements on each station.

Planning/composition

In Weeks 4 and 8 try a simple sequence linking 'like' movements together on the floor, for example, Week 4 a sequence of jumps, Week 8 a sequence of balances.

Evaluation/appreciation

Emphasis on good quality work, particularly related to jumping and balancing on floor and apparatus. For example, discussion on good landings, well-controlled balances, recognising the comparative difficulty of different balances.

(The follow-on unit could emphasise weight-on-hands and rocking/rolling activities during floor-work to continue extending movement vocabulary across the multi-activities categories. The structure of the apparatus lay-out would be different but again would be designed to encourage all five activities as the children rotate around the stations.)

Unit C – Year 2

Aim

✧ To introduce the supporting concept of using different body parts.
✧ To further understanding of the concept of sequence.

Performance

FLOOR-WORK AND APPARATUS

Using actions within the activity categories focus attention on the part of the body working the hardest:

JUMPING: legs
SWINGING: arms (pulling, suspending the body)
BUNNY JUMPING: arms (pushing, supporting the body)
ROLLING: trunk
BALANCING: variety of body parts

Apparatus lay-out design could combine pieces to encourage two different actions at each station.

Planning/composition

During the second half of this unit the children could develop short floor and apparatus sequences of actions that use different body parts, for example combining a jump and a roll. Emphasise a good start and finish, smooth joining of movements and the need for repetition to improve the quality of the work.

Evaluation/appreciation

Encourage pupils to name specific actions/skills, to identify the major body part being used, to remember the order of movements used in sequences, to recognise whether the sequence answers the task or not, to make value-judgements about the quality of their own and others' sequences.

Key Stage Two

Unit D – Year 3

Aims

- ◇ To extend movement vocabulary and understanding by applying the supporting concept of changing body shape to the five activity categories.
- ◇ To introduce the idea of performing and creating sequences to music.

Performance

FLOOR-WORK

Time is used to explore specific activity categories in relation to the concept of changing body shape. For example, jumps with different shapes, balances in different shapes, weight-on-hands activities with different shapes, rolling activities with different body shapes.

APPARATUS

A multi-activities plan with increased heights of apparatus and increased complexity in the combinations of apparatus used. Challenges in tasks encourage pupils to extend their basic actions by changing the body shape within the actions. For example, jumps with different shapes, changing shapes within a balance.

Planning/composition

In Week 4 of this block the pupils learn a teacher directed floor sequence to music. The sequence combines a jump, roll and balance in three different body shapes. The emphasis is on the phrasing of movement to the music. In Weeks 5–8 pupils select their own actions and shape-changes to construct a sequence using the same music.

Evaluation/appreciation

Emphasis on children helping each other, initially with clarity in their use of different body shapes within actions. Finally with clarity in their sequences to ensure they answer the task, and link closely with the musical phrasing.

Unit E – Year 4

Families of gymnastic skills are easily identified within each activity category (see Chapter 4). There will come a time within a well-structured, consistent gymnastics programme when primary children are ready for more specific skill-learning. Unit examples E and F will show how these can be developed within this approach, assuming the children have reached the stage of readiness for this work.

At this stage the approach might be called 'multi-skills' rather than 'multi-activities' but the skill-learning is integrated into the same basic principles of varied experiences within the five generic activity categories each lesson.

Aim

    ✦ To improve skill-learning in relation to specific gymnastic skills within each activity category, in particular attention will be focused on the weight-on-hands and rolling categories.

Performance

FLOOR-WORK

Floor-work in this half-term will focus on progressions and technical input, as required for forwards and backwards rolling, and the cartwheel weight-on-hands skill.

APPARATUS

The full range of activity categories are still structured into the apparatus plan. The weight-on-hands station will cater specifically for further practice and refinement of a range of progressive cartwheeling stages. The rolling station will cater specifically for further practice on progressive stages of forward and backward rolling.

Evaluation/appreciation

Attention will be focused on points of good technique that contribute to success in skill learning. Pupils will be encouraged to observe the work of others and assist partners with constructive corrections.

Unit F – Year 4 (follow-on example)

Aim

    ✦ To continue the development of more specific skill-learning, continuing attention on weight-on-hands skills and introducing specific balancing skills.

Performance
FLOOR-WORK

Will be used to enable practice and continued refinement of previously learned skills and the introduction of specific teaching points and progressions for the headstand balance, and the handstand weight-on-hands skill.

APPARATUS

Will still facilitate a 'multi-activities' circuit, keeping the cartwheel and rolling progressions stations from last half-term. The balance station will be made flexible enough to cater for many different stages of accomplishment with the headstand skill. One of the other stations will be designed to enable children to practise the bunny-jump/handstand in safe, progressive stages. (See apparatus plan Fig 33 for Unit F.) Such a plan might be called a 'multi-skills' apparatus lay-out.

Evaluation/appreciation

Working mainly with partners again, continuing to extend reciprocal teaching skills, encouraging skills of technical observation and constructive assistance, alongside further refinement of individual skill level.

Unit G – Year 5

Aim

✧ To extend composition skills with partners.

Performance
FLOOR-WORK

WEEKS 1–4: combining skills from different activity categories develop sequences which explore matching and mirroring with a partner.

WEEKS 5–7: explore using partners as obstacles and counter-balance ideas.

APPARATUS

Designed to facilitate partner work (see Fig 2 on page 14). Initially explore matching or mirroring ideas. Discover which actions/skills both partners can perform in unison. Later rotate around apparatus trying a range of partner ideas such as working in canon and any ideas that were successful on the floor. Partners are encouraged to explore as wide a range of actions/skills as possible.

Planning/composition

Consider the sensitivity required to work successfully with a partner. Sequences should be fluent, have a clear start and finish,

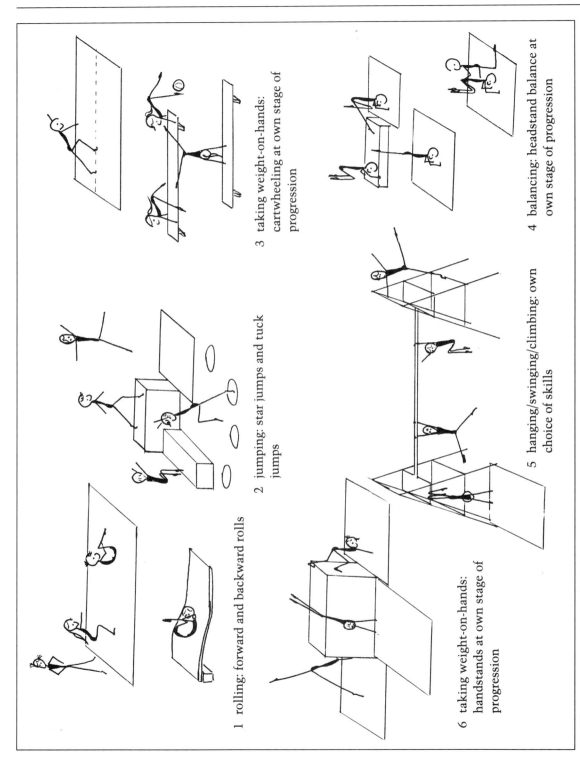

1 rolling: forward and backward rolls

2 jumping: star jumps and tuck jumps

3 taking weight-on-hands: cartwheeling at own stage of progression

4 balancing: headstand balance at own stage of progression

5 hanging/swinging/climbing: own choice of skills

6 taking weight-on-hands: handstands at own stage of progression

Fig 33   Apparatus plan for Unit F

the emphasis will be on action content and high quality performance.

Evaluation/appreciation

Discussions on the advantages and disadvantages of working with a partner. Pupils in groups of four, pairs helping each other to achieve the best possible sequences by examining factors such as accuracy in timing, synchronisation, selection of suitable moves, diversity of partner-work ideas.

Unit H – Year 6

Aim

- ✧ To encourage pupils to share responsibility for designing tasks and apparatus whilst co-operating to produce complex floor and apparatus partner sequences.

Performance

FLOOR-WORK

Pupils in pairs select their own task which must include the integration of action and supporting concepts. They can use music if the class can agree on a piece. They must record the task chosen.

APPARATUS

Classroom planning of apparatus lay-out by the pupils, all stations need to be suitable for partner-work. Pupils set an appropriate partner task for their apparatus station and select possible relationship ideas, for example, matching, mirroring, and/or canon.

Planning/composition

The pupils will be encouraged to negotiate, to contribute and share ideas, to compromise where necessary and to support each other to produce the highest quality sequences.

Evaluation/appreciation

The pupils will be encouraged to make critical judgements about their own work and the work of others. The recorded self-chosen tasks will be used to evaluate clarity of movement patterns. Pupils will be asked to comment on the appropriateness of apparatus tasks in relation to apparatus design. They will be encouraged to identify other criteria for judgements, and to apply criteria, critically and sensitively, to their own work and that of others. Video-recording would be helpful at this stage. The pupils will be invited to discuss the challenge of such an open-ended creative task.

Nine

Evaluation and assessment

In any teaching situation reflective evaluation of lessons and units, alongside formative assessment of pupil progress, are important procedures for monitoring and improving future teaching and learning. In addition, the National Curriculum requires end of Key Stage assessments in Physical Education in relation to the end of Key Stage statements. These statements constitute the statutory Attainment Target for this subject. The end of Key Stage assessments are the responsibility of every teacher.

This section contains a number of ideas to start teachers thinking about formative assessment and evaluation that will inform and improve practice, and facilitate end of Key Stage assessments.

Assessment

Time spent in any type of assessment is only valuable if the teacher is clear about:

- ✧ what is to be assessed
- ✧ who the assessment is for
- ✧ why the assessment is being undertaken
- ✧ how the results are to be used

Clearly the most valuable criteria in assessment are those that arise from the planned teaching programme. Therefore the issue of assessment must be addressed at the stage of planning the whole-school policy, the units of work and lesson plans. It is hoped that any National Curriculum criteria used in assessment arise from the Programmes of Study and that teachers will ensure these become an integral part of all planned programmes in Physical Education.

Once teachers have been realistic about what they can achieve in the gymnastics activity within the time, space and resources available, relevant assessment is possible.

Key Stage One

Using the content of the Key Stage One Units A–C described in Chapter 8, and assuming continuity of gymnastic experiences between those units, it might be reasonable to expect a seven-year-old pupil to be able to:

✧ recognise the need for certain safety requirements in gymnastics

✧ perform a broad vocabulary of simple skills in response to action tasks, for example jumping, balancing, rolling, taking weight-on-hands and hanging/swinging/climbing

✧ demonstrate movement confidence and increasing competence, particularly in relation to changing demands of the apparatus lay-out, such as different heights, surfaces and combinations of apparatus – this includes safe lifting, carrying and placing of some apparatus

✧ plan, perform, practise and improve simple sequences of movements, for example related to one activity category such as a series of rolls, or through linking two or three different actions such as jumping, rolling and balancing

✧ describe simple actions and show basic appreciation for quality of movement, for example good landings from jumps, stillness in a balance, continuity in rolling

✧ recognise the importance of warming up for gymnastics

These learning objectives, built in at the planning stage, could be used for developing pupil profiles in relation to ongoing achievement. Such a system, which plans for constant monitoring of pupils' progress in relation to learning objectives, would enable teachers to make in-depth responses to the end of Key Stage One statements. For example, it would not be difficult, with the above programme, for teachers to comment on a seven-year-old's ability to:

✧ plan and perform safely a range of simple actions and linked movements in response to given tasks (and stimuli)

✧ practise and improve their performance

✧ describe what they and others are doing

✧ recognise the effects of physical activity on their bodies

(From Key Stage One End of Key Stage Statements, Physical Education in the National Curriculum, DES 1992)

Key Stage Two

Similarly, at Key Stage Two unit and lesson planning should incorporate the criteria for end of Key Stage assessment, since they will emerge from the Programmes of Study used in the planning stage. When adapted to the possibilities within each school policy, teachers can identify realistic learning objectives to span this Key Stage.

As an example, assuming that the children have received regular gymnastic lessons throughout their junior years, including Units D–H in Chapter 8, it might be reasonable to expect an eleven-year-old pupil to:

✧ respond safely and responsibly to challenges in the gymnastic environment, for example showing understanding of the physical demands on the body, the importance of responsible behaviour and the ability to lift, carry and place all apparatus safely

✧ perform, with control, gymnastic skills within the five action categories–rolling, balancing, jumping, taking weight-on-hands and hanging/swinging/climbing

✧ explore, select, develop, practise and refine complex sequences on floor and apparatus, applying understanding of action categories, supporting concepts and partner relationship ideas

✧ evaluate performances using appropriate criteria, for example recognising the features of good technique in a skill or the qualities of good sequence work.

✧ show sensitivity to working with others, for example in adapting to a partner's skill level in planning partner sequences, in practising co-operatively, and in offering constructive criticism to improve performance

With a soundly devised programme, taught with consistency across the junior years, the end of Key Stage Two assessment should be a positive and natural culmination. For example, it would not be difficult for teachers to comment on a pupil's ability to:

✧ plan, practise, improve and remember more complex sequences of movement

✧ respond safely, alone and with others, to challenging tasks, taking account of levels of skill and understanding

✧ evaluate how well they and others perform and behave against criteria suggested by the teacher, and suggest ways of improving performance.

(From Key Stage Two End of Key Stage Statements, Physical Education in the National Curriculum, DES 1992)

Evaluation

There are many ways of reflecting on teaching and learning experiences or evaluating. There will be times for the student-teacher and teacher to reflect on many aspects of their teaching such as:

✧ the way in which they managed and organised the lesson

✧ how they structured learning

✧ the nature of their teaching style

✧ their awareness of pupils' contributions

✧ their ability to cope with the wide range of abilities within the class

✧ their success in fostering progression in learning

Evaluation of pupil-learning is an ongoing process. The teacher, through close observation, is constantly monitoring both pupils' responses and their needs for greater challenge or simplified stages of learning.

Sample methods

Example A offers a means by which the student-teacher or teacher might start to evaluate their own performance or that of their class, generally.

In addition to this continual evaluation process, the question of more specific pupil-assessment must be addressed. Example B indicates how skills identified in learning objectives for a half-term block of work could be assessed.

There might be a decision by the teacher to offer an end of year record of achievement or pupil-profile in gymnastics. This could be of value to the pupil, parent and the successive class teacher. An indication of achievement across a range of skills, needs to be based on objective assessment procedures.

There might be occasions when the teachers would like to gain an indication of how the pupils perceive their own progress. An example of one method for gaining such self-assessment is shown in Example C.

Teachers must identify those aspects of the teaching/learning experience they consider important to monitor and construct methods which are most appropriate for gaining the required information. The suggestions here are intended to offer ideas.

Example A

Evaluating teacher/student-teacher performance, and general class evaluation

Section 1: Teacher, student/teacher self-evaluation
Section 2: Evaluating pupils' progress
Sections 1 and 2 require different types of reflective evaluation.

In Section 1 teachers can reflect on how effective they were in meeting each of the criteria indicated. If the five-point scale was used over a number of lessons teachers could monitor their progress, or identify particular strengths and weaknesses.

SECTION 1
5 – extremely effective, 4 – very effective, 3 – effective, 2 – not very effective, 1 – not effective at all

1 Appearance
2 Preparation
3 Involvement/enthusiasm
4 Positioning/class awareness
5 Use of voice
6 Clarity in task-setting
7 Appropriateness of tasks for age/ability range
8 Observation skills, use of/response to work observed

9 Variety of teaching styles
10 Technical knowledge
   a Appropriate progressions
   b Correct techniques
   c Support
11 Safety
   a Organisation of pupils
   b Organisation of apparatus
   c Organisation of lesson content
12 Development of lesson
   a In format
   b In content
13 Pacing
14 Offering constructive feedback
   a To individuals
   b To the whole class
15 Positive reinforcement
16 Cognitive reinforcement, use of questioning/discussion
17 Use of demonstration
   a Purpose
   b Clarity in setting-up
   c Application of demonstration

SECTION 2
The following questions encourage reflection on pupil learning. They can be answered in a discursive way as a contrast to the method used with the five-point scale.
1 Were all the pupils challenged by the tasks set? Did they all find some success?
2 What did they learn? (About gymnastics and in addition about performance, composition/planning, appreciation skills, sharing responsibility, helping a partner, moving apparatus safely etc.)
3 Was the lesson varied, developmental and worthwhile for the pupils?
4 Did the children work within a safe, well-controlled environment throughout the lesson?
5 Was it a positive experience for the children and the teacher?
6 What are the most urgent needs of the class for the next lesson?

Example B

This is an example of a method for teacher assessment of pupil learning suitable for a class of five-year-olds:

Assessment of performance skills–ability to find varied responses to the following actions:

- *a* jumping
- *b* rolling
- *c* balancing
- *d* hanging, swinging, climbing
- *e* taking weight-on-hands

and assessment of other skills requiring the ability to:

- *f* listen and respond appropriately to action tasks
- *g* work safely with others in the hall space
- *h* co-operate with others in moving apparatus
- *i* observe and respond to simple appreciation tasks

To gain maximum information from this record teachers might wish to use a scale of differentiation. For example, the teacher could award a 5 for an outstanding response, 4 for a good response, 3 for a satisfactory response, 2 for a poor response and 1 for an exceptionally poor response.

NAME	DATE	SKILLS									OTHER COMMENTS
		a	b	c	d	e	f	g	h	i	
Vishal Karena Richard Sarah											

The teacher would need to focus his or her 'assessment attention' on a group of children in a lesson. This can be done whilst teaching the whole class. It would be impossible to make such an assessment of all pupils at once.

Clearly the skills named in this method of assessment need to be linked with the units of work undertaken. Attainment targets in physical education might be identified, as could statements of attainment from other curriculum areas, where appropriate; for example the listening skills that were identified above. It is easy to see how some of the above data could be used in pupil profiles to inform parents and pupils about their progress.

Example C

This is an example of pupil self-assessment.

Teachers could design a short questionnaire requiring pupil self-assessment after a lesson. This would enable children to reflect on their lesson and think objectively about their learning. The following might be useful for a class of ten-year-olds.

Read the sentences. Each sentence describes work you have just finished in the gymnastics lesson. Tick, against each sentence, the box which best describes how you thought you coped with the work described.

5 – you thought you coped very well
4 – you thought you coped quite well
3 – you thought you coped satisfactorily
2 – you thought you did not cope very well
1 – you thought you did not cope at all

	5	4	3	2	1
a the very energetic warm-up					
b improving your skills during the floor-work					
c helping others to set the apparatus out					
d sharing the apparatus with other children					
e making up an apparatus sequence using jumping, rolling and balancing					
f watching the work of other children and trying to help them to make improvements					

Through such a questionnaire teachers can assess pupils' perceptions of their performance, composition and appreciation skills, along with other factors such as social skills, and pupils' perceptions of their state of fitness.

Whatever means are used it is important for teachers to remember that assessment is only valuable if the teacher is clear about the purpose of the assessment and the value/use of the information collected. It must also be remembered that all that is of value cannot be assessed.

Ten

Safety in teaching gymnastics

Safe use of the gymnastics environment develops from pupils' knowledge, understanding and respect for the inherent risks of the activity. This is not to suggest that gymnastics carries any greater risk than any other area of physical education. All activities carry some inherent risks. This chapter is about minimising forseeable risks to ensure maximum safety for all participants. To ensure that risks are minimised it is necessary that codes of conduct and procedures are devised.

Pupils' attitudes towards learning in the gymnastics context are essential to safe learning and might be considered in relation to:

Respect for the teacher
In order to learn the children have to listen and respond.

Respect and responsibility for peers
This means learning to share and co-operate with others, to work together, to value the contribution of others, perhaps to support each other whilst practising a skill, to plan a sequence with a partner or to offer critical but constructive comments on a partner's sequence. It must be stressed that in order to avoid accidents, consideration of others working within the same space is vital. Careless and irresponsible behaviour cannot be tolerated because it creates forseeable risk.

Responsibility for self
Pupils need to recognise the common-sense importance of rules like 'no chewing', 'hair tied back', and adhere to them. They need to demonstrate the self-discipline to respond to a given task with appropriate and continually refined movement patterns which accurately reflect their potential.

Responsibility for the gymnastic environment
Working on large apparatus can be an exciting experience. Sharing responsibilities such as helping to move and perhaps plan apparatus lay-outs, necessitates the acceptance of certain rules and codes of behaviour. In the gymnastics lesson everyone shares responsibility for the safety of himself or herself and others.

It is the particular ethos of the gymnastics lesson, emphasised from the very start, which will enable these positive attitudes of respect and responsibility to develop. Acceptance of the necessary codes of conduct will evolve within a caring, consistent gymnastic environment.

Towards safer teaching

'Under common law, all teachers are expected to act *in loco parentis*, exercising the same degree of responsibility for the pupils in their care as would any reasonably careful parent when looking after his or her own children. This so called 'duty-of-care' exists whenever a teacher is in charge of pupils, whether or not the activity is part of the curriculum, and whether or not it takes place in school hours.'

BAALPE 1990

This general duty-of-care refers to all aspects of responsibility. In this section some very specific examples of ways in which teachers might maximise safety in the gymnastics situation will be suggested. Whilst a qualified teacher's duty-of-care responsibility can never be devolved to a student-in-training, students will always be expected to take the care appropriate to their knowledge, experience and stage of training.

Prior to the lesson the teacher can check that everyone is appropriately dressed for the lesson, if possible in bare feet, with long hair tied back and potentially dangerous jewellery removed. Obvious checks for safety in the hall will include ensuring the floor is suitable for fast moving work and that any obstacles are stacked well back on the periphery of the room. When apparatus is used the teacher ensures it is secured before the children start working.

The safest teaching will be that which results from careful planning and preparation. The best lessons will be part of a school policy for gymnastics in which the children receive continuity and consistency in their learning. Lessons should have clear aims and objectives, a structure, and attention to time which should allow for warm-up, floor-work and apparatus-work.

The teacher must monitor the whole class all the time. Deciding where to stand, or 'positioning', can create dilemmas for the teacher. It is useful to keep moving around the space in the gymnastics lesson, preferably in such a way as to keep all the children in vision, all the time. During apparatus-work it is possible for the teacher to move between stations, helping groups or individuals, whilst still ensuring that his or her positioning allows whole-class awareness. Positioning on the periphery of the room will generally facilitate this supervision. Perhaps the greatest awareness is needed when children are asked to come down from their apparatus to change stations or to watch a demonstration. At this point children should not be rushed, and teachers should ensure all are safely off apparatus before commencing with the next instruction. The monitoring of pupils' moving apparatus will be dealt with later.

Providing safe, progressive learning in gymnastics is dependent on setting tasks at an appropriate level for the pupils. This means correctly assessing the pupils' needs in relation to their stage of learning. Whilst all pupils are motivated by success, they also need to be challenged in their learning if success is to be meaningful. It might be necessary for teachers to adapt tasks for pupils with special needs. A class might contain a child who participates in a local gymnastics club and is ahead of peers in his or her learning. This child might appreciate a more complex task than the rest of the class, such as a sequencing task with three or four different demands.

With the increased integration of children from special schools into mainstream education, teachers might find pupils with a number of difficulties in their classes, for example a child with cerebral palsy. A discussion with that child's physiotherapist would be necessary prior to participation in the gymnastics lesson. It is possible that some activities would be suitable. Adapted tasks for other activities might be necessary, for example assisted jumping when other pupils were developing jumping skills.

The range of disabilities, and their implications for pupils in gymnastics lessons, is beyond the scope of this book. Teachers needing advice in this area should consult Local Education Authority Advisers, and/or seek help from local Special Schools with expertise in this area.

Teachers must also be aware of catering for any pupils with medical problems. For example, a pupil with epilepsy, who is subject to fits, should participate only with permission from the doctor and parents, and might be asked not to move high on climbing apparatus, in order to minimise risk in a fall.

Guidelines to safe use of apparatus

Key of apparatus symbols
The key of apparatus symbols on page 92 might be useful to teachers and children in the planning of an apparatus lay-out. It would need adapting to suit different schools, but such a key would ensure all teachers shared the same vocabulary for the range of apparatus available, and recognised the symbols.

Planning a 'circuit' type lay-out
The circuit is one example for a system of organising apparatus. Planning for a 'circuit' type lay-out, see Fig 1 (page 12), will require

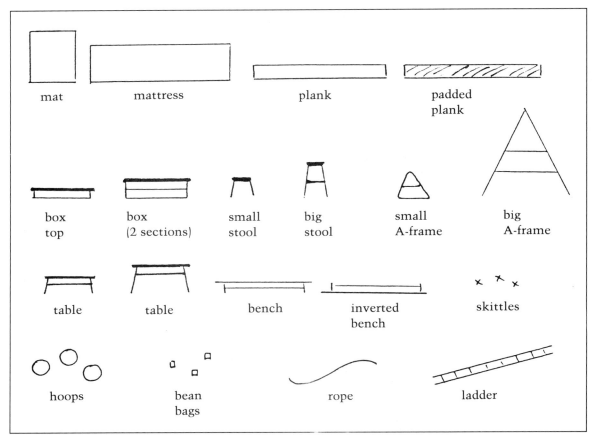

Fig 34 Key of apparatus symbols

a decision on the number of stations needed. This number will depend on class size. It is recommended that there are groups of approximately four pupils to each station, to maximise activity and avoid inactive queuing. As an example, a class of thirty-two pupils would need eight stations. Using the multi-activities approach, the teacher would plan five stations which specifically encouraged movement responses within the five activity categories. The remaining stations can be used in a number of ways. For example, tasks on two jumping stations could be differentiated so that children are asked to jump onto, along and off a bench at one whilst at the other they may be asked to show a range of jumping activities around a circle of hoops. An additional station could be allocated to the task of linking particular movements into a sequence. The movements may be directed, part directed or 'free choice'.

Rotating groups

The order of rotation of groups around a circuit will need to be considered. This is to ensure that different body parts are exercised successively. For example, it would not be beneficial for pupils to move from one weight-on-hands station to another. It would be better if they moved from jumping (legs), to balancing (different parts), to weight-on-hands (upper body, weight-supported), to rolling (trunk), to hang/swing/climb (upper body, weight-suspended).

Landing areas of each station should be carefully planned so they are away from walls, windows, obstacles, or other landing areas. Pupils will sometimes over-run a landing area and this should be taken into account.

Appropriate apparatus

The heights, widths and level of complexity of the apparatus should be appropriate for the pupils.

Links with floor-work

It will be necessary to ensure that whatever work is planned for the floor section of the lesson, perhaps
1   exploring rolling and refining the forward roll, or
2   developing the idea of moving into different directions,
can be extended on the appropriate station of apparatus.

In 1 the rolling station would be designed to allow for different stages of learning in the forward roll.

In 2 each station would have to allow for directional exploration of the action task.

Pathways

It is useful, for very young children, to establish a pathway at each station of apparatus which returns the pupils to wherever they started, see examples in Fig 1 (page 12). This organisation helps to avoid collisions between pupils, and encourages maximum activity. There are many ways to change and develop this as children mature and progress.

Use of mats

If you are in the unfortunate situation of having to prioritise where you use mats, the following guidelines might be helpful. There should be a mat:

⋄ wherever children are intended to land from a height
⋄ wherever children are intended to turn upside down

Monitoring group organisation

If the children will not rotate around all stations in one lesson, teachers will need a system of noting groups and finishing stations. The following week children can be reminded of groups, and last station. They can then progress around the circuit. Organisation of this kind is vital if pupils are to extend their physical abilities by answering the different challenges on all the stations of apparatus.

Plan or model of apparatus

It might help to have a plan or model of the apparatus lay-out in the classroom. The children could then see and discuss the stations and the related tasks. Group leaders could identify the stations they finished on last lesson, or the apparatus their group is responsible for erecting. The junior children, as they become more aware of the principles underlying the structuring of the apparatus plan, could participate in designing lay-outs for themselves. Perhaps, ultimately, groups could take responsibility, in consultation with the teacher, for designing the apparatus lay-out for a half-term block of work.

Ideas for developing the use of apparatus

There are several ways in which the teacher, and children, can develop the complexity of the apparatus, as well as several ways in which they might vary the organisation of stations from the circuit idea.

Apparatus at nursery level

If a nursery school or department has some apparatus, the multi-activities principles of encouraging movement within the five action categories can be used to plan an apparatus lay-out. As shown in many of the apparatus plans in this book, small playground apparatus like skipping ropes, quoits, hoops and bean-bags can be used as apparatus stations to encourage activities such as jumping over, along, in, out or around. At nursery level the children should be encouraged to play on the apparatus. There is much to learn from early explorations such as coping with heights, surfaces with different textures, sharing with other children, negotiating the apparatus environment and trying many different movement ideas. The basic action ideas of jumping, rolling, balancing, hanging/climbing and taking weight-on-hands can be introduced, but in a less structured manner than has been recommended for the children from reception upwards.

With reception classes

Initially reception children will respond positively to simple pieces of apparatus at stations. In the very early stages low heights of apparatus are advised for stations which might allow a 'jump off'. This is because the skill of landing safely on two feet from a height is difficult, and needs to be mastered in stages. This does not mean children cannot have higher climbing apparatus, since on these frames they can use their hands and feet to control their movements, away from, and towards, the floor. Their gripping abilities far exceed their landing abilities.

With Key Stage One classes

When the children can cope, the challenge of the apparatus can be developed. Increasing height, decreasing width, and arranging more complex combinations of apparatus will achieve this end. The teacher will need to be imaginative in trying out new combinations, different angles between pieces and different linkages. An example of how a school with one bench might use that bench, in five successive apparatus plans, to stimulate movement responses in the five different action categories, is shown in Fig 35 on page 96.

With Key Stage Two classes

Through Key Stage Two the children could contribute their ideas to apparatus planning. There is a particular challenge when trying to facilitate opportunities, at each station, to explore the supporting concepts of 'change of level' or 'pathways'. Partner-work is also a challenge to the apparatus designer since it demands consideration of matching/mirroring opportunities at each station. Fig 2 (see page 14) illustrates such a situation.

More complex sequence work will require careful apparatus planning. For example, if the class is working on apparatus sequences, which link actions from two different categories, each station would have to offer sufficient scope for the task to be met in a satisfying and worthwhile way.

There are ways of changing the challenge of apparatus by altering the pattern of use. For example, the suggested apparatus circuit, containing eight stations for a class of thirty-two children, might be completed within a two-week rotation. Another lesson might involve the children in moving continuously from one piece of apparatus to another to encourage the experience of continuity of movement. At another time, lesson content might necessitate the children staying on one station for a number of weeks to fulfil a particularly complex sequence task.

For interest, the hall space might be used in two halves. The linear nature of a longways division might be explored in the apparatus plan. A mirrored apparatus plan, within each half of a broadways division of the hall, might be a way of varying the arrangement and reducing the need for a large number of station rotations. Fig 36 on page 97 shows a mirrored plan in which four stations at one half of the hall are replicated in the other. Very basic apparatus is used to illustrate the possibility of a multi-activities plan for a school with very limited resources, and no

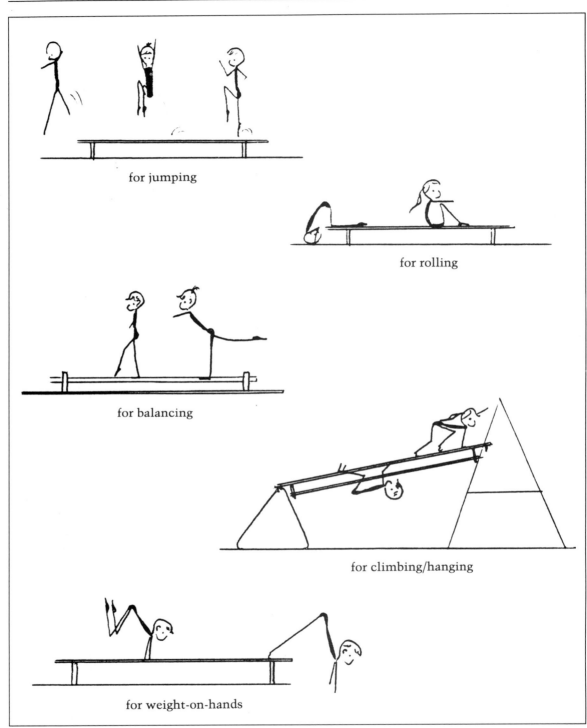

for jumping

for rolling

for balancing

for climbing/hanging

for weight-on-hands

Fig 35   Using a bench in five successive apparatus plans

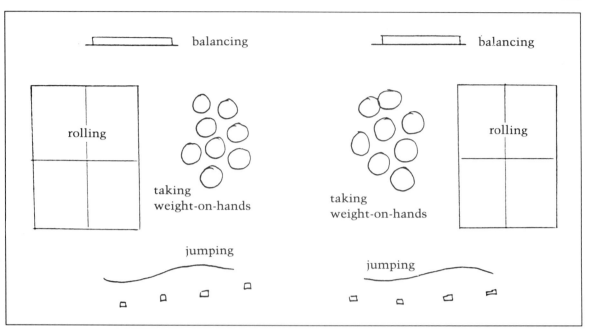

Fig 36 A mirrored plan, using symbols

facility to enable pupils to experience the hang/swing/climb movement category.

Training pupils in the moving of apparatus

Training pupils to lift, carry and place apparatus safely and efficiently is an essential part of gymnastics. Such training should be seen as a gradual process. There is no reason why teachers cannot help young children with large, cumbersome apparatus in the first instance. Children have a number of years in which to master the skills of carrying, lifting and co-operating with others, to move every piece of apparatus. A good school policy will phase in the demands of handling apparatus alongside the development of other areas of learning in gymnastics.

Safe lifting of apparatus is vital. Teachers must ensure children bend their knees, keep their backs in a normal alignment, and use their strong thigh muscles as they straighten their legs to lift. A good hand grip is essential.

Apparatus should be stored so that it is easily accessible and as close as possible to where it will be used. Pictures of apparatus or labels on walls in the places where the pieces are stored might be useful for children moving and returning apparatus. If the teachers are going to position some large apparatus then time may need to be found for this prior to the start of the lesson. Such decisions need careful planning. There will be times when training children to move apparatus takes priority in a lesson: initial steps will be slow and systematic. However, the overall balance of time in lessons should be weighted towards gymnastic activity and not apparatus moving.

Pupils should be encouraged to assume greater responsibility for moving and checking apparatus as they mature through the primary years. The final safety check is always the responsibility of the teacher. The close supervision of pupils handling apparatus is also the responsibility of the teacher. The following questions may help to break down the processes involved in safe, efficient apparatus moving.

How many children move the piece of apparatus?
For example, infants might be organised four to a mat, juniors two to a mat, perhaps two to a bench. Instructions on spacing will also help, for example one child at each corner of the mat, one at each end of the bench.

How do the children move the piece of apparatus?
Some boxes split into sections and others have wheel carriage mechanisms. Mats that are lifted, and not dragged, will last longer. If collisions are to be avoided, pupils must watch where they are going and look out for possible obstacles. A clear pathway for carrying apparatus is important. Care must be taken when returning climbing frames and ropes against the wall for securing. Flying ropes can inflict painful injury, as can boxes on wheels which are pushed too quickly and without due regard to other pupils. Lifting techniques should be checked constantly.

Where do the children place the apparatus?
If the apparatus is always stored in the same place, the children will quickly learn where to find and replace the pieces. When putting the apparatus out the teacher must be very precise over who moves what to where. The plan or model in the classroom will help. A system in which a group of pupils has responsibility for moving the same station of apparatus out and away each week, for a half-term block, would also be useful in the early stages of apparatus training.

When should the children move their piece of apparatus?
This will need organising to prevent the chaos of children carrying apparatus crossing the pathways of others. For example, if the mats are stored in one pile, a simple instruction to put the mats away might prove disastrous. Starting with the pupils holding the nearest mat to the storage pile, the teacher could successively call the names of all children with mats, giving a general task to be

performed in a space when the mat is away. This way the mats would be put away in an orderly, efficient manner, and the children would be focusing on a concluding activity rather than a mat-carrying exercise to finish the lesson.

So as to minimise risk when putting apparatus out and away:

1 Identify who will move which pieces of apparatus.
2 Remind pupils of where the pieces have to go.
3 Remind pupils of how they move their apparatus.
4 Tell each group of pupils when you want it to move with its particular apparatus. For example, the teacher might say:

I want all the mats in this half of the hall put away now, the other half clear your benches and planks.

5 Remind pupils of their responsibilities to themselves and others to tackle this sensibly and carefully.

With careful training the pupils will eventually assimilate the above points and be able to respond safely and efficiently to the simple instructions, 'apparatus out' and 'apparatus away'.

Eleven

Practical ideas for body preparation

Enjoyable exercise is motivating. In this chapter many practical fun activities, with positive gymnastic learning potential, are offered. As in all physical education contexts every lesson should begin with a warm-up. A good warm-up will set the tone of the lesson, prepare the body for work that will follow, and orientate the children to thinking in physical terms. The selection of content material for the warm-up will depend upon many factors, such as the age and experience of the children and the nature of the teaching space available.

One way in which to structure the warm-up is to break it into two parts. The first part would consist of a fast-moving introductory activity. The second part would include some appropriate physical conditioning activities, that is those which help with strengthening or flexibility of the body. These qualities are essential to safe, efficient learning in gymnastics, therefore this section can be linked with the skill-learning work to follow.

The first past of this chapter describes a number of introductory fast-moving activities. The best way to channel the initial release of energy which greets the start of gymnastics lessons is with an activity which is simply organised and involves the use of the whole body. These activities may, or may not, take a game form and there are many hundreds which would be suitable.

The second part deals with physical preparation. This section of the warm-up concentrates on exercising the joints and the associated muscle groups in preparation for the demands that subsequent gymnastic activity will make on them. The activities used should ensure that joints are worked through their entire range, gently but firmly. Some strengthening exercises for the main muscle groups may also be included. The teacher's approach to the exercises, the type of exercises and their duration will vary depending upon the age of the children and the objectives of the teacher.

Introductory fast-moving activities

Using music

Musical 'statues'
Music suitable for skipping or gentle jogging is played. Each time the music is stopped the children immediately adopt a pre-determined position or shape. (Note the potential for the early teaching of basic gymnastics language and rhythmic training in this game.) The game could become 'musical shapes' or 'musical positions'.

    Variation: the adopted shapes could be sequenced so that when the music is first stopped a star shape is used, on the second stop a tucked shape, etc. This obviously requires a very basic movement memory. 'Musical balances' is another possibility and 'Musical body-parts'. If there is limited space this can be an effective, energetic, worthwhile, on-the-spot warm-up.

Musical changes
Music is selected which suits particular loco-motor activities such as jogging, skipping, jumping, hopping, striding, etc. A cassette tape should be made up, containing 10-15 second snatches of different music. As the music changes then so does the mode of locomotion.

    Variations: clearly there are many variations available and tapes can be 'tailor made' to suit the motor skill level of the particular class.

'Capture' or penalty games

'Stick-in-the-mud'
Two children are chosen to be 'on'. They run and chase the others who when 'tagged' (touched) assume the pre-determined 'caught' position, say a tightly tucked sit on the floor. In order to be released back into the game one child who is 'free' must, say, astride jump over one 'caught' or put a hand on his/her head and run a complete circle around him/her without breaking contact.

    Variations: the variations to this game are countless. The capture positions may be varied, as may be the means of making free.

Fig 37
'Stick-in-the mud'

'Chains'
One child is selected to be 'on'. He/she chases the others until one is touched. They then join hands and the chase resumes until another is caught. This makes a chain of three. The next one caught starts another chain and so on until everyone is caught. (Note – it is not advisable to have chains longer than three.)

Fig 38   'Chains'

'Slow Sam'

Children sit in a space. On the command 'GO' they touch lines near the outside of the space on all four sides of the room and return to sit in their place. The last two or three back receive a 'penalty', say five tuck jumps. It is important that teachers do not use 'exclusion games' in which the last ones back sit out, since the intention is to provide an effective physical warm-up for everyone.

Variations: as well as changing the starting and finishing position it is possible to lengthen the game, and thus the physical demands, by sequencing the runs. Each time the starting place is reached a certain task may be required, for example holding a front support position for a count of ten, balancing on one foot for a count of ten, doing five tuck jumps, before setting off on the run again.

'Groups'

Everyone skips or jogs around the room until a number is called out. Groups of the size corresponding to the number called are formed and then they sit down back to back. Anyone left out or those in wrong sized groups pays a penalty, say stepping or jumping on and off a bench at the side ten times.

Variations: many variations of this basic game are possible and two examples are given. The constitution of the groups may be fixed, say one boy and two girls or two girls and two boys. This variation achieves a better 'mixing' effect and the potential for 'catching' more people out. The finishing position may be changed, say two standing and two sitting. Those groups in error pay the penalty. Clearly the demands made can be adjusted to the age and abilities of the class.

'Pairs races'

The children sit back to back in pairs. On a command one assumes a front support position. The other then jumps over his/her outstretched legs, say ten times before changing place.

Fig 39   'Pairs races'

They race the other pairs to complete the task before returning to their starting position. The last pair to finish receive a penalty.

Variations: the limit to the number of variations to this activity is dependent upon the imagination of the teacher.

Relay races

Relay races are popular games used as introductory activities for the older children. However, it is important that the races take a form which ensures that the children are all active most of the time.

Continuous relays

(These can be enjoyed by classes of sensible children who understand the need for responsible behaviour to ensure the safety of others.)

One basic form of this game is as follows:

Equal sized teams of not less than six are formed. Each team lines up, one behind the other using the whole length of the available area. The team adopts the starting position, say straddle stand. On

leap frog

tucked sit

front and
back support

Fig 40   Continuous relay

being given the command to start the one at the front moves to the back of the line through the outstretched legs. Having gone through everyone else's legs he/she now turns round and runs back along the outside of the line, not back through the legs again, to his/her starting place and stands in straddle stand position. As soon as the first person has gone through the legs of the second in line the second person then closely follows the first. Once they have both cleared the third then the third tags on to the end of the line and follows number two. This continues until they are all back in their original places. If the sequence is not broken then each member of the team will have been through everyone else's legs.

Variations: there are many variations available in the starting position such as front support, back support, tucked sitting, and much gymnastic vocabulary that can be taught through this game. The positions will, of course, alter the action demands on those negotiating them, for example children might be asked to jump over the feet in the front support positions or to run a circle, with hand on head, around each tucked sitting person. Returning home actions can also be varied, for example running could be hopping, jumping, tuck-jumping, scrambling on hands and feet, etc.

Sequential relays

Small teams of three or four line up one behind the other at one end of the available space. On starting the race the first team member runs to a pre-determined spot (a line, mat, hoop) and performs, say, ten tuck jumps before running to the next point where, say, ten bunny jumps would be required. As soon as the

Fig 41   Sequential relay

first station is vacated the next team member may start and similarly with the next team member. This continues until each member of the team has visited each exercise station in turn.

Variations: the possible variations are obvious. The number of exercise stations and what is required at each may be changed. The teacher could also stipulate the means of moving from one station to the next such as jumping, hopping, hands and feet.

Physical preparation

It is impossible to describe all the exercises which are suitable for inclusion in this section, there are just so many. Teachers should 'collect' examples of suitable exercises and build up a personal 'bank' which may be called upon when required. Such knowledge would ensure variety in the exercises selected to achieve specific effects.

Careful selection of activities could reinforce concepts, or offer practice opportunities in certain aspects of performance. Alternatively the activities could be used to help strengthen certain muscle groups or develop flexibility in joint complexes which could, in turn, aid the acquisition of particular skills.

Game/Exercise 1 'Sticky legs'

One pupil sits or lies on the floor with legs straight and tight together. He/she tries to keep the legs together as a partner attempts to pull them apart at the ankles.

Fig 42   'Sticky legs'

Objectives
✧ To strengthen the muscles which help keep the legs together when performing certain skills.
✧ To 'educate' the muscles in this particular role.

Carry over
Reference to the muscle action/game can be made as pupils practise such skills as shoulder stand, log roll, forward roll, swinging, 'V' sit.

Game/Exercise 2 'Pat-a-feet'

Partners sit opposite each other and, with legs bent, work out a clapping sequence with their feet. (Similar to a hand-clapping game.)

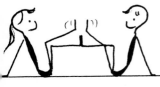

Fig 43   'Pat-a-feet'

Objective
✧ To help strengthen abdominal muscles.

Carry over
Abdominal strength helps maintain the tucked position in forward rolls, tucked hang on a bar, tucked jumps.

Game/Exercise 3 'Crossed lines'

Pupils take up a front support position with hands on one side of a line. On the signal they 'jump' or 'walk' their hands together backward and forward over the line a set number of times whilst maintaining a straight body, i.e. no bending at the knees. The first to complete the number of 'jumps' and then sit down is the winner.

Objective
⋄ To help strengthen the muscles of the upper body and abdominal muscles.

Carry over
The exercise will help develop the strength required for weight-on-hands activities and the muscles of the trunk for body tension.

The examples offered below are in a 'fun activity' form. With young children this type of activity is generally more acceptable than formal exercises. However, exercises of a formal nature, for example press-ups, sit-ups, could be used to reinforce a 'Health Related Fitness' project or focus, whilst fulfilling the role of this section of the warm-up.

Using a ball

Fig 44   'Roll-a-ball'

'Roll-a-ball'
Sit in wide straddle with legs straight. Roll the ball as far forward as possible without bending legs. Keep both hands on the ball. Do this several times trying to go further each time. (Stretch for hamstrings and lower back.)

'Bridge ball'
Lie on the back with body fully stretched. Lift hips up high to make a bridge. The ball is passed under the bridge and the back returned to the floor before the ball is then rolled under bent legs. (Back, buttocks, hamstring and abdominal strengthener.)

Fig 45   'Bridge ball'

Fig 46   'Circle ball'

'Circle ball'
Sit in pairs back to back, legs straight and together. Ball is rolled around making as big a circle as possible on the floor. (Stretch for hamstrings and lower back.)

Fig 47   'Twister ball'

'Twister ball'

Children stand with feet apart, back to back with approximately 1¹/₂ metres between them. Keeping both hands on the ball and arms straight the ball is passed around them to the left, say, ten times before repeating to the right. (Trunk twisting.)

'Over/under ball'

Teams of four/five standing with feet apart in a line about 1¹/₂ metres from each other. With each person keeping arms straight, and both hands on the ball, the ball is passed alternately overhead and under between straddled legs until the ball reaches the back of the line. The person at the back now runs to the front and repeats the sequence. The line gradually advances until a particular line is passed. (Extension and flexion of spine, hamstring stretch.)

Fig 48   'Over/under ball'

'Stretcher ball'

Teams of four lie on the floor stretched out in a line with fingers just touching heels of next person. Last person holds the ball and swings arms and ball upwards and over head to sit up at the same time straddling the legs and reaching forward to give the ball to the next team member. This is repeated until the ball is received by the person at the front who sits up and reaches the ball as far along the floor as possible. The sequence is now repeated in reverse with each team member lying down in turn to pass the ball back to the start. Teams can repeat this a set number of times as a race. (Abdominal muscles strengthener plus hamstring and and lower back muscles stretcher.)

Fig 49   'Stretcher ball'

Games using a bench

'Tunnel bench'

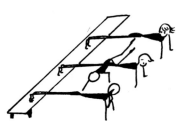

Teams of, say, five make a tunnel by assuming a front support position with feet on bench and hands on floor. The end pupil crawls under the bridge then runs back to his/her place. The next in line repeats this by running to one end of the bridge and crawling to the other. This continues until everyone has gone under the bridge and assumed the starting position. (Strengthening of abdominal, and upper body support muscles.)

Fig 50   'Tunnel bench'

Variations: the shapes used to form the tunnel may be varied depending upon the physical effects required, for example:

1 Front support with hands on bench and feet on floor (physical demands are less strenuous than the earlier example).
2 Bridge (spine and shoulder extension).
3 Back support (back and shoulder muscle strengthener).

Fig 51   Variations on 'Tunnel bench'

'Jumping bench'

Teams of, say four sit astride a bench. On the signal everyone must jump on to the bench, turn around then jump astride and sit down again. This is repeated a number of times. The whole team goes together. The winning team is that in which every member has completed the required number of jumps first. (Leg muscles strengthener with cardo-respiratory effects.)

Variations: the many variations are obvious. The desired physical effects determine the particular tasks set.

Games without apparatus

'Flippers'

From a half squat position the children jump as high as possible. Whilst in the air they try to clap the soles of their feet together. The class could 'race' to see who would be the first to do, say, ten claps. Alternatively the target could be a series of jumps during which one clap is made, then two, then three and so on to see who can go the furthest. (Leg strengthener.)

Fig 52   'Flippers'

'See-saw'

One pupil sits on the floor in a tight tuck position and holding the hands of a partner who stands in front. The standing partner assists the other to stand by giving a little pull which moves the sitting partner's weight from seat to feet. As one partner rises to stand the other sinks to sit. The action is repeated rhythmically much in the fashion of a 'see-saw'. Whilst this sounds a simple activity it is quite difficult to achieve a steady rhythm, especially if the stipulation is added that each time one sits the heels must be lifted off the floor. (Leg strengthener.)

Fig 53   'See-saw'

'Caterpillars'

From a front support position the pupil progresses between two points, for example across the room or from one line to another, by moving first feet, then hands. The arms and legs must be kept straight the whole time and the feet walk in to end as close to the hands as possible. This way the distance is covered in as few 'close ups' as possible. (Hamstring stretch and shoulder strengthener.)

Fig 54   'Caterpillars'

'What's the time?'

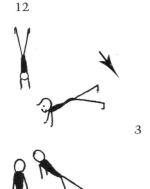

From front support with the hands in the middle and the legs pointing at 12 o'clock on an imaginary clock face, the pupil moves, keeping body and legs straight, to point his/her feet at the hour called by the teacher. In this activity the pupil moves through front, back and side support positions. Thus 12 o'clock is represented by front support, 6 o'clock by back support, 3 and 9 o'clock by side support on the right and left hands respectively. (Shoulder, abdominal and back muscles strengthener.)

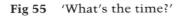

Fig 55   'What's the time?'

Fig 56   'Rock 'n Roll'

'Rock 'n Roll'

Lying on their backs the pupils slide their fingers down their thighs until they can just touch their knees. In this 'dished' position with chins on chests they rock forwards and backwards. When the teacher signals 'roll' they put their arms above their heads, roll over to an unforced arched back position as quickly as possible and continue rocking forwards and backwards on their tummies. Each time the teacher gives the signal the children roll over. Shoulders and feet should not touch the floor at any time. This is a very demanding exercise but most useful for developing body tension. (Abdominal and back muscles strengthener.)

'Lift the log'

Children are asked to find a partner about their own size. One lies flat on the floor with hands on thighs and tries to maintain a straight, tight shape as the other lifts his/her feet from the floor. (Back and hip extensor strengthener.)

Fig 57   'Lift the log'

'Front support lift'

This is similar to 'Lift the log' but the starting position is a front support. Again a straight, tight body shape should be maintained as the feet are lifted from the floor. It is important that the lifter takes care not to pull the partner's shoulders from immediately above his/her hands. (Abdominal and shoulder muscles strengthener.)

Note: The above two activities are ideal for the teaching of correct lifting techniques. As much attention should be paid to this aspect as to the maintenance of the correct body shape.

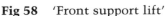

Fig 58   'Front support lift'

'Stubborn donkey'

Pupils choose a partner about their own size. One takes up an 'all-fours' position with legs straight and straddled. The partner now tries to push or pull the 'stubborn donkey' from the spot. (Develops body tension.)

Fig 59   'Stubborn donkey'

'Turn the turtle'

One pupil takes up a shape on the floor. The partner simply tries to turn him/her over. The starting shape, once assumed, must be maintained. The easiest version of this game is for the 'turtle' to remain perfectly straight with legs together and arms above the head. A tucked shape is also fairly easy to turn over. The wider the legs and/or arms are spread, the more difficult the task becomes both for the partner to turn the body over and for the 'turtle' to hold the body shape. (Develops body tension–may also be used to illustrate and/or practise lifting techniques.)

Fig 60   'Turn the turtle'

Gymnastics in the primary school should be part of a balanced programme of physical education. Teachers will decide, within a school policy for the subject, how much time children will spend on gymnastics, dance, games, athletics, swimming and outdoor and adventurous activities. For some of those aspects, such as dance and outdoor education, it is not difficult to see how learning experiences might be linked with projects extending across the curriculum. The desirability of linking learning experiences is well-accepted within primary education. In this final chapter the potential of learning in gymnastics being linked with other areas of the curriculum will be explored.

As stated in the introduction, the value of gymnastics, as an activity worth pursuing for its own sake, is the chief justification for its place in the primary curriculum. As shown throughout this book, children can be guided in progressive learning of performance skills, planning/composition skills and evaluation/ appreciation skills. Through a structured programme children will develop a physical confidence which will enhance their lives. They will understand movement differently, be more physically able, be more aesthetically perceptive, more informed about the movement they watch and more sensitive to the needs and abilities of others. For these reason children should be entitled to gymnastics in education.

The National Curriculum for England and Wales sets out to ensure all pupils receive a curriculum of entitlement. Through the multi-activities approach to teaching gymnastics, the requirements of the attainment targets and the programmes of study for gymnastics can be met. In relation to the rest of the curriculum there will be times when learning in gymnastics can link very well with learning in other subject areas. There will be other times when making unsuitable links, for the sole objective of forcing the whole curriculum to fit into a particular topic package, would be positively detrimental.

Primary teachers are in the best position to decide when and where cross-curricular links are desirable and feasible. Examples are suggested of ways in which learning in gymnastics might be linked with other National Curriculum areas, when and where appropriate.

English

The attainment target of speaking and listening contains many skills which might be met through the teaching of gymnastics. Clearly the children have to listen if they are to learn; following instructions is vital to safety in gymnastics. The skills of appreciation, discussed in Chapter 6, involve children in speaking, answering questions, describing movements observed, communicating, reflecting on work, expressing and justifying opinions on their own work and that of others, with increasing sophistication. All of these skills are mentioned under the speaking and listening attainment target in the English curriculum documentation.

Science

Some National Curriculum attainment targets such as 'Processes of life,' 'Forces,' and 'Energy', all have content material which could be considered during gymnastics lessons. For instance, a project on the body might coincide with a half-term block of gymnastics work based on the multi-activities approach, with the supporting concept of 'body parts'. The teacher could reinforce classroom learning on identifying and labelling different body parts, by making this the core of attention in gymnastics.

'Forces' might be explored in gymnastics by asking the children to consider practically which forces produce and prevent movement, for example pull/push, gravity/friction. With a good gymnastic warm-up children should certainly feel themselves getting hotter, and they would learn the importance of raising the body temperature prior to stretching the muscles. Such practical experiences might be useful in a project on 'Energy'.

Mathematics

There could be opportunities in gymnastics for young children to reinforce their learning about number. For instance, they could increase their understanding of cardinal number by responding to tasks like:

Show me four jumps, show me eight hops.

Similarly, gymnastics might be used to reinforce the concept of ordinal number with tasks like:

The first movement in our sequence is a jump, the second is a roll and the third is a balance.

Sally's mat is going away first, John's second, Ashwin's third, Lynn's fourth and Lucy's fifth.

When working on defining sets children have to develop their abilities to define attribute characteristics. The multi-activities approach is based on the understanding of five different types of movement. Early learning must involve finding appropriate criteria for sorting actions into these five categories. For example: what makes a roll a roll, a balance a balance, or a jump a jump?

Perhaps when the children are learning about repeating patterns they could reinforce this with simple sequencing in gymnastics. The teacher could demonstrate a simple repeating pattern, for example straight jump–tuck jump, straight jump–tuck jump. The children could then contribute their own ideas for sequences with simple repeating patterns. The number of actions can be increased to develop the complexity of the task.

Many aspects of shape can be reinforced in gymnastics.

Performing and recognising shapes, perhaps specific gymnastics shapes like straddle and pike, can be added to work in the classroom on recognising shape. Symmetry might be an aspect of shape which coincides with a block of gymnastics work in which symmetry and assymmetry are explored in relation to the five action categories.

Spatial concepts like on, off, over, under, around, are ideally explored in gymnastics, for example, with weight-on-hands activities along a bench. Learning rights and lefts, and turning through right-angles, quarter and half turns can also be practically explored in gymnastics. For example, a jumping warm-up could be a set sequence of jumps which included quarter and half turns to the right, to be repeated to the left. This is always fun and can be quite complex depending on the length and order of the sequence.

Technology

In the chapter on safety, the planning of apparatus was considered in detail. The possibility of involving children in generating designs was suggested. This might coincide with work in technology on designing. Children would enjoy using their ideas to make a plan of a possible apparatus lay-out, based on an understanding of the basic principles of the multi-activities approach.

At a later stage children might be involved with producing their own design specifications demonstrating increasing awareness of the need for safety in relation to gymnastics at all stages. There is no doubt, if pupils are given the chance to put their plan into action, that they would enjoy discussing the results with their teacher and peers and analysing how successful their plan was for the class.

The above examples indicate ways in which it might be possible to link teaching and learning in gymnastics with core areas of the curriculum. The primary teacher must make choices about when and where those links would be most valuable and meaningful for their pupils.

Health Education

Finally, some aspects of the cross-curricular theme of health education can be reiterated although they underpin most of the contents of the book.

Throughout this book gymnastics has been shown to have a particular role to play as a medium for educating young people about the importance of all-round exercise. Learning in gymnastics necessitates attention to body posture, efficient ways of moving the body, and correct techniques of lifting, supporting and carrying. Through participating in gymnastics young children can begin to understand the importance of strength and flexibility in developing healthy bodies and in successful skill-learning. Such knowledge will enhance the development of appreciation skills as children understand how these fitness factors relate to the aesthetic nature of gymnastic performance.

The health education perspective on safety has also had a very high profile throughout the book. Educating young children to accept responsibility for the safety of themselves and others, in the gymnastic environment, has been stressed as the most essential feature of good teaching from the very first lesson.

In relation to developing positive attitudes to an active life-style, enjoyable, successful experiences in gymnastics will result in enthusiasm, self-confidence and a desire for further participation, as in any area of learning. Positive attitudes to physical education should be evident throughout a school. They are reflected in the attitudes of staff, pupils, the state of facilities and equipment, in a balanced programme of physical education for all children and often in some extra-curricular opportunities or links with local sports centres.

Gymnastics is just one context of movement education which should be offered to children in an exciting and challenging programme of physical education. The most important time in life to be exposed to this varied and challenging movement education is in the primary years. It is hoped that this book will encourage some teachers to provide a progressive, enjoyable, challenging gymnastics programme for their children.

References

Introduction

1 MAWER, M. and HEAD-RAPSON (1985): 'Professional courses in
   Physical Education for non-specialist primary and middle school teachers'
   (pages 14-21); *Physical Education within Primary Education*
   A volume of essays compiled by the Primary School Study group of the
   Physical Education Association.
2 WRIGHT, J. (1991): 'Gymnastics – Ideals for the 1990's?' (pages 8-14);
   British Journal of Physical Education 22:3

Chapter 1

3 SMITH, Bob (1989): 'Schools Gymnastics. Guidelines for Teaching' (pages
   132-134); *British Journal of Physical Education* 20:3
4 BAALPE (British Association of Advisers and Lecturers in Physical
   Education) (1988): *Gymnastics in the Secondary School Curriculum*
   (Booklet and video); White Line Press, Leeds
5 DEPARTMENT OF EDUCATION AND SCIENCE (1978):*Primary
   Education in England* (page 69); HMSO
6 WARBURTON, P.A. (1989): 'Barriers to progress in Primary School:
   Physical Education' (pages 165-166); *British Journal of Physical Education*
   20:4
7 CLARKE, M. (1982): 'The Value of Gymnastics in Education' Gymnastics
   in Education Conference Papers, Liverpool Polytechnic
8 UNDERWOOD & WILLIAMS (1991): 'Personal and Social Education
   through gymnastics' (pages 15-19); *British Journal of Physical Education*
   22:3

Chapter 6

9 BEST, D. (1988): 'The Aesthetic in Sport'; *Philosophic Inquiry in Sport*
   Eds. W.J. Morgan and K.U. Meier, Human Kinetics, Illinois

Chapter 10

Recommended further reading

BAALPE (1990): *Safe Practice in Physical Education*, particularly the
   sections on Gymnastics, and Physical Education for pupils with Special
   Educational Needs
COLLINS, V. (1988): 'Negligence and physical education' in 'Legal liability
   and Physical Education' conference proceedings (pages 3-4); Carnegie
   Department, Leeds Polytechnic,
   2 Nov 1988
WEARMOUTH, H.(1990): 'The prudent coach: legal considerations' (pages
   49-61); *BAGA Women's Gymnastics Manual* Colin Still, Springfield
   Books Ltd, Huddersfield